C000263663

SEARCH FOR THE WORLD'S BEST BARTENDER

This book is dedicated to my mum, dad and brother, from my heart.

Erik Lorincz

On July 15, 2010 Erik Lorincz of the Connaught Hotel in London was crowned Diageo Reserve's 2010 World Class Bartender of the Year. The title is the ultimate prize in bartending, and represents the culmination of a year-long search for an individual that personifies modern mixology, complemented by some of the finest spirits ever produced: Johnnie Walker Blue Label Blended Scotch Whisky, Tanqueray No. TEN gin, Ketel One vodka, Don Julio tequila, Cîroc vodka and Zacapa® rum.

Some 24 countries competed this year, with each nation holding its own multi-stage competition to identify those with the greatest cocktail prowess. From a massive 6,000 entrants, the 24 national champions were then pitted against each other in a four-day international final, facing a series of challenges that tested every aspect of the bartending profession.

This year's international final was held in Athens, the home of last year's winner, and united young and emerging talent with some of the biggest names in the global bartending community: again, thanks to judges Salvatore Calabrese, Peter Dorelli, Gaz Regan, Dale DeGroff, Hidetsugu Ueno and Alberto Sorias.

Congratulations to Erik: winning World Class is truly life-changing and we wish him well as he embarks on what is surely to be an epic year, not least in international travel, to showcase his particular brand of creativity to the world as a World Class ambassador.

As ever, it's been a privilege to be part of World Class, to experience the cutting edge of bartending expertise and witness how the initiative is driving cocktail culture globally. Next year, we're looking forward to even more countries participating as the journey continues.

Cheers
Simon Difford

Search for the world's best bartender DIAGEO RESERVE 2010 (ISBN: 978-0-9556276-8-2) is published by Odd Firm of Sin Limited, 1 Futura House, 169 Grange Road, London, SE1 3BN, England. www.diffordsguide.com.

Design, words and photography by Odd firm of Sin
Odd Firm of Sin Limited and Diageo Plc specifically disclaim any implied warranties of merchantability of fitness for a particular purpose. The advice and strategies contained herein may not be suitable for your situation. Johnnie Walker® Gold Label™ Blended Scotch Whisky, Johnnie Walker® Blue Label™ Blended Scotch Whisky, Johnnie Walker® Green Label™ Blended Scotch Whisky, Tanqueray® No. TEN™ gin, Don Julio® tequila, Cîroc® vodka are all registered trademarks of Diageo. Zacapa Centenario, Zacapa Centenario logo and Zacapa Centenario bottle are all trademarks of Rum Creation & Products, Inc. The Grand Marnier word and associated logos are owned by Société Marnier Lapostolle. Ketel One and Ketel One Citreon words and associated logos are trademarks of Double Eagle Brands N.V. All other trademarks are the property of their respective owners and are used in this publication under licence.

THE
FINALISTS

Timo Janse

Representing: The Netherlands
Head Bartender at Door 74, Amsterdam
Age: 29

Despite studying economics at the University of
Amsterdam, Timo always wanted to be a bartender,
and found part-time work first at what he describes as
a "party bar" and then at the College Hotel in
Amsterdam, where the staff were inspirational
bartending teachers.

Abandoning the idea of pursuing economics as a
career, he bought one of Gaz Regan's books and
started entering cocktail competitions. Undeterred by
an initial losing spell, he persevered and was named
Dutch magazine Venuez' Best Bartender 2009, before
winning Bols Around the World competition and
finally World Class for Holland.

Smokey Papa Don

Glass: Old Fashioned
Garnish: Long grapefruit twist
Method: SHAKE first four ingredients with ice and
strain into ice-filled glass. FLOAT Ardbeg on drink.

2 shots Don Julio Reposado tequila
¾ shot Marmalade/chili syrup (heat two kilos of sugar
with one kilo of warm water and add 10 sliced chillis.
Allow to simmer for 15 minutes then add 1 ½ litres of
grapefruit marmalade and 1 ½ litre of orange
marmalade)
¾ shot Fresh pink grapefruit juice
¾ shot Freshly squeezed lemon juice
2 dashes Lagavulin 16 Year Old Scotch Whisky

Alcohol per serving: 9.4g

Torsten Spuhn

Representing: Germany
Owner of Modern Masters Bar & Lounge in Erfurt
Age: 42

Torsten left school with plans to be a journalist before briefly pursuing a career in costume jewellery. But he was destined to work in a bar and started out in the industry as a glass washer and bar-back. By the age of 20 he was a bar manager, but struggled with F&B managers who blocked his ideas and he longed to open his own bar.

In 2001, he achieved his dream when he opened Modern Masters, Erfurt, a small town between between Frankfurt and Berlin. Often nominated for German Bar of the Year, Modern Masters is noted for its cuisine-style drinks, classics and 80s drinks.

The Grey Flannel

Glass: Martini
Garnish: Pink grapefruit zest twist
Method: SHAKE all ingredients with ice and fine strain into chilled glass.

⅔ shot Tanqueray No. TEN gin
1 spoon Mandarin marmalade (with bits)
⅔ shot Earl Grey tea
4cm fresh Lemongrass

Alcohol per serving: 9.3g

Amanda Wan

Representing: Malaysia
Bartender at Vintage Banks, Hilton, Kuala Lumpur
Age: 24

Amanda wanted to be an artist but at art school she was pushed towards graphic design. Disenchanted, she found herself working at Starbucks where she became fascinated how different coffee beans and roasting methods could produce such different flavours. She then moved on to a wine bar, where her new-found interest in flavours exploded, and mixology was a natural extension.

Her mother persuaded Amanda to only work in the bar part-time so she could return to education: for her final year's dissertation she wrote a study on the evolution of mixology up to the 21st century. Her rapid progression and win of Malaysian World Class is perhaps partly attributable to her bar supervisor and mentor, who was actually last year's Malaysian winner of World Class.

One Last Straw

Glass: Martini
Garnish: Mandarin orange peel
Method: SHAKE all ingredients and fine strain into chilled glass.

1½ shots Ketel One vodka
1 shot Condensed milk
1 shot Balsamic vinegar
Fresh Strawberries
Strawberry preserve
Sugar syrup

Alcohol per serving: 7.1g

Adam Brewer

Representing: Australia
Bartender at Sling Lounge, Brisbane, Australia
Age: 23

Adam grew up in Tenterfield, a town in New South Wales with a mere 2,700 inhabitants. He couldn't wait to escape and moved to Brisbane as soon as he was 18, working part-time as a bartender while studying for a double degree in law and business.

With a mother who was a restaurant manager, Adam grew up with an understanding of the service industry and had always thought about becoming a bartender. He finally committed fully to his calling at Brisbane's Sling Lounge – technically a tapas restaurant, but also regarded as one of Australia's best cocktail bars. Adam has previously competed in several cocktail competitions, winning a local Brisbane competition organised by Diageo before winning the Don Julio tequila Margarita Challenge and qualifying for World Class.

The Aristocrat Stinger

Glass: Martini
Garnish: Lemon twist discarded, charcuterie board and grated bitter chocolate
Method: STIR all ingredients with ice and strain into chilled glass.

1⅓ shots Lagavulin 16 Year Old Scotch Whisky
⅓ shot White crème de menthe
⅓ shot Pedro Ximénez sherry
2 dashes Chocolate bitters

Alcohol per serving: 8.7g

Erik Lorincz

Representing: UK
Bartender at The Connaught Hotel, London
Age: 30

Erik began his bartending career in 2000 in his native
Slovakia, before relocating to Prague and London,
working at seminal members club Attica. He began as
a bar-back but his natural talent quickly shone
through and he rose to become head bartender. Stints at
Japanese restaurant Nozomi and The Sanderson Hotel
followed before he started at The Connaught in 2008.
His theatrical presentational style has already helped
him win a host of national competitions in the UK.

"I almost didn't make it to Greece," he said on the
eve of the competition. "I broke my front teeth after I
banged my head in a friend's wine cellar and have
been in agony. I collapsed at the hospital and have
been on morphine – and now I'm on antibiotics so I
can't actually drink alcohol at the moment! I think
this will be my most luxurious week ever. But now I'm
here, face-to-face with the crème de la crème of the
bartending world, and I want to win this
competition."

Rising to the sky

Glass: Martini and small tumbler for botanical steam
Garnish: Botanical steam (Macerate coriander,
juniper, grapefruit peel in hot water then pour over
dry ice.)
Method: SHAKE all ingredients with ice and fine
strain into chilled glass.

1½ shots Tanqueray No. TEN gin
⅓ shot Yuzu juice
¾ shot Freshly squeezed lemon juice
½ shot Pressed pineapple juice
⅓ shot Fino dry sherry
½ shot Sugar syrup
8 fresh Coriander leaves

Alcohol per serving: 9.0g

Thomas Huhn

Representing: Switzerland
Bartender at Les Trois Rois, Basel
Age: 34

A bartender for 13 years, Thomas began working in his native Germany before working on cruise ships and doing stints at the Hyatt International and Kempinski groups of hotels. His current home, Les Trois Rois, is a five-star hotel bar specialising in cognac, with a fine cigar collection – though he says success at World Class depends on a wide spirits and cocktail repertoire.

"You need all your bartending skills to compete in World Class – you need to know your cocktail history, but also to be able to create new style cocktails, and the best part of that is in being able to meet your heroes, like Salvatore Calabrese, and take your new ideas back to your bar."

The Flying Dutchman

Glass: Absinthe glass
Garnish: Salt and lemon pepper rim, orange twist
Method: Put absinthe-soaked sugar cube on absinthe spoon over glass and ignite it. SHAKE remaining ingredients and strain into absinthe glass filled with ice cubes. Serve with absinthe spoon in glass.

⅔ shot French absinthe
2 shots Ketel One vodka
⅔ shot Freshly squeezed lemon juice
3 cubes Sugar
1 shot Egg white

Alcohol per serving: 14.8g

Tomas **Dundulis**

Representing: Dubai
Bartender at Okku, The Monarch, Dubai
Age: 26

Tomas is from Lithuania, but honed his bartending skills in London at TGI Fridays – renowned for training a generation of bartenders – and the Living Room W1 before relocating to the Middle East and Okku, a contemporary bar and VIP lounge.

"In Dubai people like anything that's expensive: they love cash and they love to show off. There are a lot of good cocktail bars there, but sometimes it's hard to find a bar that's really creative, inventing their own new drinks. I'm looking forward to meeting new people – Dale DeGroff is the sort of person I look up to – someone who's published his own books and comes up with new stuff which I can use to help me in my goal of having my own bar. Eventually I'd love to take all this knowledge back to Lithuania."

Mexican Red

Glass: Coupette
Garnish: Passion fruit boat and Himalayan rock salt rim
Method: MUDDLE passionfruit, lemons and limes in base of shaker. Add other ingredients, SHAKE with ice and fine strain into chilled glass.

2 wedges Lime
2 slices Lemon
1 fresh Passion fruit
⅔ shot Don Julio Reposado tequila
½ shot Triple Sec liqueur
⅓ shot Caramel syrup
⅛ shot Vanilla syrup
½ shot Passion fruit purée
½ shot Raspberry purée
⅛ shot Freshly squeezed lemon juice
⅛ shot Freshly squeezed lime juice

Alcohol per serving: 5.4g

Richard Gillam

Representing: Singapore
Bar Operations manager at New Asia Swissôtel,
Singapore
Age: 31

A truly international bartender, and a competition
veteran, Richard has worked in bars across the UK
and consulted for new bars in New York, Thailand and
the Maldives, focusing both on bar operations and the
physical design of underbars. He has taught
bartending at the Shaker Schools in the UK and even
designed his own glassware range.

His career is a complete contrast to the
cybernetics and robotics he studied at university, but
he says it put him on the path to analysing how
systems works – which he has put to good use behind
the bar.

"Throughout my career I've tried to pass my
knowledge back – for me, World Class is not just
about winning but demonstrating what I've learned
and taking it back to Singapore, which is still a
developing cocktail market. For my signature serve
I've been working with a specialist tea maker to create
a blend that perfectly complements Tanqueray No.
TEN gin."

T in a Teacup
Glass: Martini
Garnish: Mandarin orange zest twist
Method: SHAKE all ingredients with ice and fine
strain into chilled glass.

2⅔ shots TWG Tea-infused fresh grapefruit juice
2 shots Tanqueray No. TEN gin
1⅓ shots Fresh pomegranate juice
⅔ shot Egg white
1 twist Grapefruit zest

Alcohol per serving: 14.9g

Heinz Kaiser

Representing: Austria
Bar manager at DINO's American Bar, Vienna
Age: 43

Heinz is competing at World Class with a plaster cast on his left arm, having injured his little finger. Despite being told at one point that he risked losing the use of his finger, he's on the road to recovery. One of our oldest competitors, he combines a 20-year career in bartending with practising as a professional pharmacist, which he says gives him a unique insight into how flavours in alcoholic drinks marry together – and which has contributed to an obsessive attitude to food and drink.

"I'm not able to pass any food, Asian or Indian store without looking for new flavours, and I can't eat anything without thinking about turning it into a drink. It rules my life. I make all my own syrups, infusions and bitters, and I'm going to be using my own Earl Grey tea bitters in my signature drink."

Gimlet Caprese

Glass: Martini
Garnish: Balsamic reduction inside glass, skewer with baby mozarella and cocktail tomatoes
Method: Lightly MUDDLE basil with cracked pepper and vodka in base of shaker. ADD other ingredients, SHAKE with ice and fine strain into chilled glass.

2 to 3 grains Long pepper (Java, Indonesian or Piper Longus pepper)
3 to 4 Basil leaves
2⅔ shots Ketel One vodka
1 shot Freshly squeezed lime juice
⅔ shot Sugar syrup

Alcohol per serving: 12.6g

José Luis León Martínez

Representing: Mexico
Bartender at Hotel Distrito Capital, Santa Fe
Age: 22

José Luis has been working as a bartender for four years, making him our youngest finalist, and is fairly new to the competitions scene – though he recently performed in Cuba. He's found a niche for himself behind the bar after starting his career in construction.

"I'm not nervous – though I am anxious to learn from the people here, as I want to work as a bartender for a long time. I try to work with any spirit, not just tequila – mixing flavours is the most interesting part of bartending. I'm most looking forward to the speed round, as my bar is very busy and it will be good to see how quickly I can make good drinks."

Ketel Fresh

Glass: Martini
Garnish: Grape, celery and lemon twist
Method: MUDDLE fruit and mint in base of shaker. Add other ingredients, SHAKE with ice and fine strain into chilled glass.

2 shots Ketel One vodka
8 fresh Seedless green grapes
4 fresh Mint leaves
1 shot Freshly squeezed lime juice
1 shot Celery juice
1 spoon Caster sugar

Alcohol per serving: 9.5g

Felipe Navarro

Representing: Colombia
Bartender at Club El Nogal, Bogota
Age: 27

Felipe is proud to be representing his country and feels it is on the cusp of a major change in cocktail culture.

"I want to share what I have learned in Colombia and take back the knowledge I acquire in Athens – feeding back different cocktail cultures to each other. Cocktails are already popular in Colombia and a level of general knowledge definitely exists, but it is missing some aspects and molecular mixology has to be further developed."

Felipe works at Club El Nogal, one of the most upmarket social clubs, located in a vast sports, leisure and entertainment establishment with numerous restaurants and bars in the centre of Bogota. He was actively supported by the sommeliers and other bartenders who work there in his preparation for World Class.

Grape Trilogy
Glass: Martini
Garnish: Grape and kidron leaf
Method: SHAKE and strain in chilled cocktail glass.

1 shot Cîroc vodka
1½ shots Grape infusion (infuse 500ml water with "Isabelina" grapes and kidron)
½ shot Sugar syrup

Alcohol per serving: 4.7g

Arnaldo Hernandez

Representing: Puerto Rico
Bartender at the InterContinental San Juan Resort &
Casino, San Juan
Age: 37

Arnaldo couldn't make it to World Class last year
because his young daughter was suffering from back
problems – but now that he's here, he's out to make
his mark. "I've got lots of tricks up my sleeves. I'm
trying to do with vodka what my country has always
done with rum. I've brought lots of fruits typical to
Puerto Rico for infusions and flavours and that's
something that's going to be a big surprise."

Mystery Moon

Glass: Martini
Garnish: Mango and nectarine
Method: MUDDLE ginger, passionfruit, coriander
and brown sugar in base of shaker. Add other
ingredients, SHAKE with ice and fine strain into
chilled glass.

1 piece Root ginger
½ fresh Passion fruit
4 fresh Coriander leaves
2 spoons Brown sugar
2 shots Ketel One vodka
½ shot Triple sec liqueur
2½ shots Ruby red grapefruit juice

Alcohol per serving: 11.8g

Max La Rocca

Representing: Ireland
Bartender at Sheen Falls Lodge, Kenmare, Co. Kerry
Age: 38

When it comes to jobs, you name it and Massimo La Rocca has probably done it. He's worked in restaurants at London's Harrods and Claridge's, DJ'd in Italian wine bars and owned a web agency. Now very much settled behind the bar and enjoying his time in Southern Ireland, he's finally found his ideal career.

"You've got to leave a mark on your guests before they leave your bar," he explains. "Throughout everything I've done, every role I've held, there are these very Italian threads: delivering something unique that involves all the senses and creates a real feeling of family."

A Mermaid in the Bush River

Glass: Old Fashioned
Garnish: Orange twist
Method: THROW (strain form vessel to vessel to mix) all ingredients with ice and strain into ice-filled glass.

1⅛ shots Bushmills 16 Year Old Irish Whiskey
⅓ shot Aperol bitter
⅓ shot Cherry brandy liqueur
⅛ shot Orgeat (almond) syrup
1 dash Angostura aromatic bitters

Alcohol per serving: 7.1g

Ilias Marinakis

Representing: Greece
Bartender at Baba Au Rum, Athens
Age: 23

This is Ilias' first ever cocktail competition and he is keen to follow in the footsteps of last year's winner, Greece's Aristotelis 'Telis' Papadopoulos.

"When I get behind the bar at Baba Au Rum, I feel like I'm home," he says. "They're my friends there – I love bartending so much I'd work for free! Just don't tell my boss…"

Monroy

Glass: Brandy Snifter
Garnish: Pink grapefruit zest twist (discarded) and shiso leaves
Method: DRY SHAKE all ingredients (without ice) and strain into glass.

2 shots Tanqueray No. TEN gin infused with shiso leaves
½ shot Rooibos tea
½ shot Freshly squeezed lime juice
⅓ shot Honey
2 dashes Grapefruit bitters

Alcohol per serving: 11.2g

Richard **Gonzalez**

Representing: Dominican Republic
Bartender at Cava Bar Lounge & Martini Lab,
Santo Domingo
Age: 33

It's not often you meet a bartender who was originally
training to be a pilot – especially one who's done
everything from parking cars in Puerto Rico to
running a 107-strong 'martini lab' in the Dominican
Republic in between.

"The cocktail in the Dominican Republic is really
up-and-coming. They're very creative back home for
sure, but I had a bit of an edge from my experience in
the States."

Don Julio Spectrum

Glass: Martini
Garnish: Cardamom powder and sugar rim,
dehydrated mango slice, curaçao and grenadine down
the inside of the glass
Method: BLEND mango purée, coriander, lime juice
and brown sugar syrup, then SHAKE and fine strain
into chilled cocktail glass.

2 shots Don Julio Reposado tequila
¾ shot Pomegranate liqueur
1½ shots Mango purée
1 shot Freshly squeezed lime juice
1½ shots Brown sugar syrup (mix ½ cup brown sugar
with ⅓ cup hot water)
5 fresh Coriander leaves
1 dash Grenadine syrup
1 dash Blue Curaçao liqueur

Alcohol per serving: 10.8g

Rina Fermin

Representing: Venezuela
Bartender at Suria, Valencia
Age: 35

Rina's first experience of the bar industry was washing glasses at a friend's bar in Venezuala at the tender age of 16. Almost 20 years later, she can't imagine being anywhere else but behind the bar.

At World Class Rina is taking a distinctly creative, spontaneous – and philosophical – approach to her cocktails. "This is us," she says, "We're bartenders. We taste something and the ingredient tells us what it wants to be, not what we want it to be. It's like when you're carving a stone: the art is already in there, waiting inside. It's a passion and it's an art, and if you don't believe in it –if you don't have that passion – then don't do it."

La Coa

Glass: Martini (7oz)
Garnish: Cucumber and star fruit slice
Method: MUDDLE star fruit in base of shaker. Add tequila and cucumber juice, SHAKE with ice and fine strain into chilled glass. Separately SHAKE triple sec with ice and carefully fine strain so layer floats on top of cocktail.

3 fresh Star fruit slices
1½ shots Don Julio Reposado tequila
1½ shots Cucumber juice
1 shot Triple Sec liqueur

Alcohol per serving: 11.5g

Noach Van Damme

Bar: L'Apereau, Blankenberge, Belgium
Representing: Belgium
Age: 27

A former forklift-truck driver, Noach has been working as a bartender at L'Apereau for five years, helping take it from a general bar to a specialist cocktail bar – regarded as one of the best in Belgium. Largely self-taught, this is the second year running he has represented Belgium in World Class – a first for the competition – with a co-worker at his bar coming in second, for the second year running too.

What Noach likes about mixology is its ability to surprise drinkers, he says. "Belgium doesn't have a cocktail history or culture, so it's great to be able to introduce people who don't necessarily think about spirits much to the cocktail world. We started with easy drinking cocktails, such as the Mojito, but now are customers are growing with us and drinking Martinis and Sazeracs."

Aqua Regia (King's Water)

Glass: Old Fashioned
Garnish: None
Method: SHAKE ingredients except milk with ice and fine strain into glass. FROTH milk and layer on top of drink.

1⅓ shots Johnnie Walker Gold Label Blended Scotch Whisky
1 shot Pedro Ximénez sherry
⅔ shot Speculaaslikeur (gingerbread-like liqueur by Weduwe Joustra)
1 dash Jerry Thomas bitters
1 dash Old Time aromatic bitters
1 sheet Gold leaf (aprox. 8x8cm)
Milk (Friese Vlag, Lang Lekker)

Alcohol per serving: 11.1g

Esteban Delgado Badilla

Representing: Costa Rica
Bar: T.G.I. Friday's, San José
Age: 32

TGI Fridays played a pivotal role training a generation of bartenders in the UK, and Esteban says it is now playing a similar role in Costa Rica. A bartender for four years, he was working as a waiter in a restaurant when the customers he was serving – who turned out to be TGI Fridays' managers –offered him a job.

He hasn't looked back – learning from a venue that he says is undisputedly the best bar in Costa Rica. And despite making a mean Margarita and perfecting Long Island Iced Teas – the drinks TGIs is famous for – he has a penchant for aged spirits and really pushing the boundaries of drinkers' perceptions. "I make the most crazy stuff," he says. "I roast strawberries and mix them with whisky, I love cooking and working with chefs, and I like the challenge of creating new drinks, particularly with dark spirits."

Hi Class Cocktail

Glass: Old Fashioned
Garnish: Rose petals
Method: POUR first two ingredients into glass. SHAKE other ingredients with ice and fine strain into charged, ice filled glass.

1 shot Tanqueray No. TEN gin
1 dash Green melon liqueur
1 shot Johnnie Walker Blue Label Blended Scotch Whisky
1 shot Don Julio Reposado tequila
1 splash Sour mix
1 splash Hi Class Mix
"Hi Class Mix" (combine water, sugar, lemon and orange peel, cinnamon, strawberries, ginger, rose petals and pieces of black oak, then cook together)

Alcohol per serving: 15.0g

Takumi Watanabe

Representing: Japan
Chief Bartender at The Sailing Bar, Kibi, Japan
Age: 38

Takumi, which translates as "authentic craftsmanship", studied law but loved his part-time bartending job so much that he decided to give up college and become a full time bartender. Now with 19 years' experience, Takumi has been the chief bartender at The Sailing Bar in Kibi since it opened in 1994.

The Sailing Bar is a small intimate members' bar that holds a mere eight guests but incredibly employs half that number – three bartenders and one chef. Although bijou, The Sailing Bar offers a full French and Italian menu, and boasts an extensive wine list – Takumi is a trained sommelier. As well as wine and food matching, Takumi matches cocktails to dishes – indeed cocktails dominate sales.

Botanical Garden

Glass: Martini
Garnish: Zest of sudachi (Japanese lime) cut in the shape of a butterfly
Method: SHAKE all ingredients with ice and fine strain into chilled cocktail glass.

1 shot Tanqueray No. TEN gin
⅔ shot Green tea
½ shot Fresh Sudachi (Japanese lime) juice
⅛ shot Sugar syrup
1 fresh Shiso leaf

Alcohol per serving: 5.6g

Jordi Otero

Representing: Spain
Mandarin Oriental, Barcelona
Age: 30

Jordi has been bartending for 12 years, opening his
first bar when he was just 21 and using his
international travel experiences as a foundation for
his approach to drinks. But while he enjoyed the
independence of running his own place, he says it's
his experience at the Mandarin Oriental in Barcelona,
where he works closely with chefs to concoct new
ingredients and flavour pairings that has truly
inspired him.

He says he's part of a cocktail revolution in
Barcelona, with drinkers more willing to experiment
than ever, particularly with his own signature
infusions and pairings. "It's far easier than it used to
be to find a bar in Barcelona that can make great
cocktails," he says. "There's a new generation of
drinkers who used to just order a whisky and soda:
now everyone is travelling more and discovering a
new world."

Purple Emperor

Glass: Shot
Garnish: Jasmine leaves and Comté cheese
Method: INFUSE rum and cold tea for two minutes,
then stir and strain into glass.

1 ⅔ shots Zacapa 23 rum
⅓ shot Elderflower liqueur
⅛ shot Jasmine tea

Alcohol per serving: 8.7g

Angus Zou

Representing: Taiwan
General manager at Marquee Restaurant & Lounge,
Taipei
Age: 27

When it comes to its consumer drinks scene, Taiwan might not have the kind of hunger for classics and molecular concoctions that runs rampant throughout much of the West. Combined with the fact that Angus Zou had never touched a drop of alcohol before getting behind the bar, you might be forgiven for wondering what he's doing at a cocktail competition. But with early training from the likes of Angus Winchester and Dale DeGroff, and a clearly long-term love for the industry, it all becomes clear.

"With only four years behind the bar, my techniques might not always be the best. But being a cocktail bartender in Taiwan takes patience and self-belief. As a bartender, I can give something very special to people. And maybe they can give me something special back. I think that's very cool."

Martini Reviver

Glass: Old Fashioned – Tea cup
Garnish: French bread with crushed olives, dash of balsamico on top
Method: TOAST bread, then pour Ketel One vodka through it into mixing glass: add Green Chartreuse inside, stir until chilled and strain into glass /cup.

2 shots Ketel One vodka
2 dashes Green Chartreuse liqueur
1 piece French bread

Alcohol per serving: 7.9g

Maxime **Hoerth**

Representing: France
Bartender at the Four Seasons, Hotel George V, Paris
Age: 24

Almost every ounce of Maxime's education has
focused on the drinks world. He's studied hotel
management and catering in Strasbourg for six years,
has put in time behind bars in Switzerland and Paris,
and is now relishing the challenge of working with
such a prominent company as Four Seasons.
"I'm young and I'm creative but I have less experience
than some of the other competitors. But because I'm
young I'm also less restricted by the old rules. I love
working with fresh ingredients and am looking
forward to showing what I can do."

From Paris, With Love
Glass: Martini
Garnish: None
Method: MUDDLE celery and grapefruit, add other
ingredients, SHAKE and fine strain into chilled
cocktail glass.

1⅔ shots Tanqueray No.TEN gin
10cm fresh Celery
⅛ wedge Pink grapefruit
1 spoon Rose's lemon and lime marmalade
⅓ shot Freshly squeezed lime juice
2 dashes Grapefruit bitters

Alcohol per serving: 9.7g

Rafael Pizanti

Bar: Head bartender, Bar Do Copa, Copacabana Palace Hotel, Rio de Janeiro
Age: 27

Rafael's career as a bartender is something of a departure from his childhood dream of becoming an archaeologist, but he's now pursuing a profession that he's passionate about. After studying hotel management in his home city of São Paolo, he first took a position as a bar-back in an Italian restaurant, then worked as a barista and took roles in several restaurants in the city and Rio de Janeiro.

Rafael is looking forward to his next career move with his current employer: he hopes to become Executive Bartender, responsible for three bars in the hotel's ocean-front complex. He also harbours a longer-term ambition to tend bar overseas, building on his already excellent spoken English.

Bitter Sweet Martini

Glass: Martini
Garnish: Orange twist
Method: SHAKE and fine strain into chilled cocktail glass.

1¾ shots Tanqueray No. TEN gin
¾ shot Licor 43 liqueur
⅛ shot Aperol bitter
1¾ shots Freshly squeezed grapefruit juice

Alcohol per serving: 12.7g

Do-Hwan Eom

Representing: Korea
Bar Captain at The Ritz, Seoul
Age: 34

Do-Hwan Eom began working as a bartender at The Ritz in Seoul in 2000 – 10 years later he's proud still to be leading the way there. For the first round of World Class, he took on almost 150 of his fellow Korean bartenders to make it to the semi finals, and another 30 at the next round, to make it to the international finals here in Athens.

"The best thing about being a bartender," he says, "is getting to meet so many different people from so many different countries and backgrounds. But in return as a bartender, it's vital that we can make customers comfortable – that we can crack a smile and make them enjoy themselves. And this is what I do best."

Shall We Kiss?

Glass: Martini
Garnish: Torched barley bread with chestnut honey and fresh thyme
Method: SHAKE and fine strain into chilled cocktail glass.

2 shots Cragganmore Single Malt Scotch Whisky
⅓ shot Chestnut honey syrup
½ shot Freshly squeezed lemon juice
1 shot Egg white
1 dash Citrus bitters
Red ginseng
Fresh thyme

Alcohol per serving: 9.5g

DIAGEO RESERVE®
WORLD CLASS
RAISING THE BAR

ATHENS 2010

THE
CHALLENGES

Cocktail Mastery

The World Class Cocktail Mastery segment challenges World Class competitors to deliver not just on their drinks-making ability – but on the power of their palate.

Each was required to distinguish 20 aromas from a list of 40 commonly found in spirits, to blind taste and identify four brands from a chosen category of four spirits – distinguishing between a competitor brand, a supermarket brand, a different Diageo product and the Diageo Reserve brand – and to answer 20 multiple-choice questions on a spirit category of their choice.

They were then charged with making two cocktails, one classic (with any twist they liked to give), the other a wholly original creation.

As such, it was a test of the all-round capabilities demanded by modern mixology amid an ever-expanding market of products. Held at Balthazar, a large open-air bar in central Athens, our finalists faced seasoned drinks pro Gaz Regan across the bar – putting competitors at ease with his friendly and easy-going nature that belies an encyclopaedic knowledge about cocktails, drinking culture and professional bar service.

> **1 Shot = 15ml / ½ ounce**

Tomas Dundulis
Dubai

Mexican Red (signature)
Glass: Coupette
Garnish: Passion fruit boat and Himalayan rock salt rim
Method: MUDDLE passion fruit, lemons and limes, add other ingredients, SHAKE and fine strain into chilled glass.
⅓ shot Don Julio Reposado tequila
½ shot Triple Sec liqueur
1 fresh Passion fruit
2 wedges Lime
2 slices Lemon
⅛ shot Freshly squeezed lemon juice
⅛ shot Freshly squeezed lime juice
½ shot Passion fruit purée
½ shot Raspberry purée
⅓ shot Caramel syrup
⅛ shot Vanilla syrup
Alcohol per serving: 5.4g

Sweet martini (classic)
Glass: Martini
Garnish: Orange twist
Method: STIR vermouth with ice then discard excess, leaving vermouth-coated ice, then pour vodka over, stir and strain into a chilled glass.
1⅓ shots Cîroc vodka
⅛ shot Sweet vermouth
Alcohol per serving: 6.5g

Tomas kept his martini deliberately simple, but was keen to bring out the citrus flavours of Cîroc vodka, preferring an orange twist to lemon, which he said was too dry and sour for the sweeter style of martini he was making. He described stirring cocktails as the bartenders' equivalent of fishing, taking him to a quiet place of contemplation – perfect for coming up with new recipes.

Recreating his signature, winning drink that won him the title of World Class Dubai winner, Tomas emphasised that his twisted Margarita must include a sea salt rim to balance the drink. "The Margarita should be a sour drink," he says. "It has to be sea salt – you get something extra coming through.

Erik Lorincz
United Kingdom

Rising to the Sky (signature)
Glass: Martini for cocktail and a small metal tumbler for the botanical steam
Garnish: Botanical steam on the side
Method: SHAKE with ice and fine strain into chilled glass. Serve with botanical steam on the side.
1½ shots Tanqueray No. TEN gin
⅓ shot Yuzu juice
¾ shot Freshly squeezed lemon juice
½ shot Pressed pineapple juice
⅓ shot Fino dry sherry
½ shot Sugar syrup
8 fresh Coriander leaves
For the Botanical Steam: coriander, juniper, grapefruit peel macerated in hot water and poured over dry ice
Alcohol per serving: 9.0g

Tanqueray No.TEN martini (classic)
Glass: Martini
Garnish: Lemon zest twist
Method: STIR all ingredients with ice and strain into chilled glass.
3 shots Tanqueray No.TEN gin
½ shot Dry vermouth
3 dashes Camomile bitters
Alcohol per serving: 17.9g

Erik twisted a traditional gin martini with his own homemade camomile bitters – made from a base spirit of Tanqueray No. TEN gin and designed to perfectly complement the flavours of the gin. And to create some extra theatre, he used hand-chipped ice from a slow-frozen block he had brought in especially for the competition, stirring the gin, vermouth and bitters in a rare stemmed mixing glass before throwing it.

"It's all about the details," he says. "Just as we care about our guests, we care about our ice. You can see that the block of ice is very dry, so when you are using it with martinis it adds a real texture to your spirit. And when it comes to the martini there must be theatre as it's the most 'economic' of cocktails. There's no point just simply adding all the ingredients to a mixing glass or putting everything into a shaker – that's why we created the martini trolley at The Connaught."

Finally, he used a magician's technique to 'disappear' his lemon twist after he had spritzed the surface of his martini.

Adam Brewer
Australia

Ruby Tuesday (signature)
Glass: Coupette
Garnish: Grapefruit zest twist
Method: SHAKE all ingredients with ice and fine strain into chilled glass.
1⅓ shots Don Julio Blanco tequila
½ shot Freshly squeezed lemon juice
½ shot Fresh pink grapefruit juice
½ shot Homemade chilli and tarragon syrup
⅓ shot White crème de cacao
⅓ shot Raspberry liqueur
⅛ shot Egg white
Alcohol per serving: 8.0g

Bullfighter (classic)
Glass: Martini
Garnish: Lemon zest twist
Method: STIR all ingredients with ice and strain into chilled glass.
1⅓ shot Don Julio Reposado tequila
½ shot Sweet vermouth
⅓ shot Grand Marnier liqueur
1 dash Anise liqueur
Alcohol per serving: 8.9g

Adam's signature drink, the Ruby Tuesday, was his tribute to the 20th Century Cocktail – a gin-based mix of crème de cacao, Lillet Blanc aperitif wine, lemon juice and egg white. He twisted it with grapefruit juice, homemade chilli and tarragon syrup and raspberry liqueur to create a delicately textured drink with a slight kick.

For his classic drink Adam used the combination of sweet vermouth and Pernod to recreate the flavours of a now defunct vermouth – Hercules – listed as an ingredient in this classic cocktail in 1937, resulting in an incredibly smooth and silky cocktail. The remainder of the drink he poured from his mixing glass into a miniature flask cocooned in iced water for further tableside theatre.

Esteban Delgado Badilla
Costa Rica

Best Class (signature)
Glass: Flute
Garnish: Orange zest twist
Method: MUDDLE strawberries and rose petals, then add syrup, cinnamon, fruit juices and tequila. Flambé in mixing glass; add whisky and gin, SHAKE with ice and fine strain into flute.
¾ shot Don Julio Reposado tequila
¾ shot Johnnie Walker Blue Label Blended Scotch Whisky
¾ shot Tanqueray No.TEN gin
½ shot Fresh orange juice
1½ shots Freshly squeezed lime juice
2 Large strawberries
6 Rose petals
1 shot Sugar syrup
1 dash Cinnamon powder
Alcohol per serving: 11.1g

Margarita (classic)
Glass: Tumbler
Garnish: Salt rim around half the glass
Method: SHAKE all ingredients with ice and strain into ice-filled glass.
¾ shot Don Julio Blanco tequila
¾ shot Don Julio Reposado tequila
1 shot Freshly squeezed lime juice
1 shot Sgar syrup
½ shot Triple Sec liqueur
1 dash Grand Marnier liqueur
Alcohol per serving: 9.7g

Estaban began his presentation in an unconventional way, presenting Gaz Regan with a rose before making his cocktails. Whether he was flattered or not is unconfirmed, it was actually part of preparing his signature drink, which saw him muddling rose petals and strawberries with gin, tequila and whisky. It made for easy drinking.

Estaban was unusual among World Class bartenders in freepouring all his ingredients – a method he also used for his classic cocktail, a Margarita. "That's the way I do it," affirmed Gaz, who was pleased with the finished result.

Richard Gillam
Singapore

T in a Teacup (signature)
Glass: Martini
Garnish: Mandarin orange zest twist
Method: SHAKE all ingredients with ice and fine strain into chilled glass.
2⅔ shots TWG Tea infused fresh grapefruit juice
2 shots Tanqueray No.TEN gin
1⅓ shots Fresh pomegranate juice
⅔ shot Egg white
Grapefruit zest
Alcohol per serving: 14.9g

Gin Flip (classic)
Glass: Flute
Garnish: Lemon zest spritzed over the finished drink then discarded; also uses a light dusting of nutmeg or cinnamon depending on the time of day
Method: SHAKE all ingredients with ice and fine strain into flute.
2 shots Tanqueray No.Ten gin
2 shots Fresh pink grapefruit juice
⅔ shot Sugar syrup
One whole egg
Alcohol per serving: 11.2g

For his T in a Teacup, Richard combined Tanqueray No.TEN gin with his own blend of Tanqueray-flavoured tea, which he had created in conjunction with the TWG tea company's master blender, and presented in a specially created Tanqueray/TWG-branded caddy.

He shook the drink in a crystal shaker before serving it in a crystal martini teacup he had designed himself, and garnished the drink with grapefruit marshmallow squares dusted in coriander and liquorice sugar, and his own-baked juniper muffins. Richard described the result as a twisted Clover Club, combining the best of Singapore and British culture.

Richard chose a Gin Flip for his classic cocktail, which he said evoked past times but tended to be overlooked. He decided to forgo the option of a dry shake: "When you mix it up with ice the whole thing lightens up and becomes really fresh."

Rafael Pizanti
Brazil

Bitter Sweet martini (signature)
Glass: Martini
Garnish: Orange zest twist
Method: SHAKE all ingredients with ice and fine strain into chilled glass.
1¾ shot Tanqueray No.TEN gin
¾ shot Licor 43
⅛ shot Aperol bitter
1¾ shot Fresh grapefruit juice
Alcohol per serving: 12.7g

Dry martini (classic)
Glass: Martini
Garnish: Olive stuffed with almond and lime zest rubbed around the rim
Method: STIR ingredients with ice and strain into chilled glass.
2 shots Tanqueray No.TEN gin
⅛ shot Dry vermouth
Alcohol per serving: 11.5g

Rafael's simple and straightforward approach to bartending meant for a speedy and efficient delivery. He chose what he said was one of the best examples of classic cocktails which judge Gaz Regan said really woke him up. Meanwhile, his signature serve of a Sweet martini with fresh ginger, raspberry and apple juice won the reward from Gaz: "This is a beautiful drink."

Maxime Hoerth
France

From Paris, With Love (signature)
Glass: Martini
Garnish: None
Method: MUDDLE celery and grapefruit, add other ingredients, SHAKE with ice and fine strain into chilled glass.
1⅔ shot Tanqueray No.TEN gin
10cm Fresh celery
⅛ wedge Pink grapefruit
1 spoon Rose's lemon and lime marmalade
⅓ shot Freshly squeezed lime juice
2 dashes Grapefruit bitters
Alcohol per serving: 9.7g

Andrea's Clover Club (classic)
Glass: Martini
Garnish: Lemon zest twist
Method: SHAKE all ingredients with ice and fine strain into chilled glass.
1⅔ shots Tanqueray No.TEN gin
⅔ shot Freshly squeezed lemon juice
⅓ shot Rose syrup
2 barspoons Raspberry purée
½ Egg white
2 barspoons White sugar
Alcohol per serving: 9.3g

For his signature serve, Maxime had his feet firmly planted in his own home country. Named after a John Travolta film (no, us either) Maxime said he had chosen to include a vegetable he didn't actually like because he admired the complexity it can bring to a drink. "I don't like celery at all but was having a boring day at work and was playing with the ingredients we use for Bloody Marys. The celery brings a real vegetal and spicy taste to the drink."

Gaz Regan commented: "It's a very complex drink, and I liked how the celery garnish forced me to inhale the flavours too."

Do-Hwan Eom
Korea

Shall We Kiss (signature)
Glass: Martini
Garnish: Torched barley bread with chestnut honey and fresh thyme
Method: DRY SHAKE ingredients then shake again with ice and fine strain into chilled glass spritzed with bitters.
2 shots Cragganmore Single Malt Scotch Whisky
Red ginseng
1 sprig Fresh thyme
⅓ shot Chestnut honey syrup
½ shot Freshly squeezed lemon juice
1 shot Egg white
1 dash Citrus bitters
Alcohol per serving: 9.5g

Rob Roy (classic)
Glass: Martini
Garnish: Maraschino cherry
Method: STIR all ingredients with ice and fine strain into chilled glass.
1 shot Johnnie Walker Gold Label Blended Scotch Whisky
⅔ shot Sweet vermouth
1 dash Angostura aromatic bitters
Alcohol per serving: 6.7g

Korea's finest created high expectations from the start. Followed by a Korean TV crew throughout the competition, Do-Hwan laid out bar-top equipment including gold tongs, barspoon, strainer and jigger; various atomisers, an infra-red thermometer and a make-up brush. Tasting his lemon juice to test its acidity, and storing his jigger in water, Do-Hwan manifested the precise and deliberate techniques east Asian bartenders have become renowned for.

Do-Hwan chose thyme to complement what he said he felt was a principal herbal note within Cragganmore Single Malt Scotch Whisky. A dry shake preceded a wet shake, then the mixture was poured into a martini glass that Do-Hwan had sprayed with his own homemade citrus bitters. A garnish of barley bread, spread in chestnut honey and thyme leaves completed the signature serve. "Incredible," said Gaz Regan.

Jordi Otero
Spain

To Naftaki (signature)
Glass: Martini
Garnish: Basil leaf
Method: SHAKE all ingredients with ice and fine strain into chilled glass.
2 shots Don Julio Añejo tequila
1 shot Tawny port
1 shot Freshly squeezed lime juice
½ shot Homemade vanilla syrup
10 Basil leaves
1 whole Egg white
Alcohol per serving: 11.4g

Margarita (classic)
Glass: Flute
Garnish: None
Method: SHAKE all ingredients with ice and fine strain into chilled glass.
2 shots Don Julio Reposado tequila
1 shot Grand Marnier liqueur
1 shot Freshly squeezed lime juice
1 whole Egg white
Alcohol per serving: 13.7g

Jordi, distinct in the uniform of Barcelona's Mandarin Oriental, his bar equipment in a sleek metal case, and large, expensive looking glassware on the bar, looked like he meant business from the start.

But straight away, he informed judge Gaz Regan that he was an old-school bartender in his heart and that his drinks would reflect that: "I'm keeping it simple," he said. "I'm not a fan of molecular mixology. I want to make you something you drink. I hate 'eating' cocktails."

His To Naftaki cocktail, meaning 'little sailor' in Greek, was designed to be redolent of the sea. "I'm from Barcelona and when I smell this drink I remember the sea. People think I'm crazy to use añejo tequila but I think that's what works best."

His twist on a margarita was to include egg white. "I think it gives you a little more balance as well as texture."

Torsten Spuhn
Germany

Temptation (signature)

Glass: Tumbler
Garnish: Lemon, thyme and pink grapefruit twist
Method: STIR all ingredients with ice and fine strain into ice-filled glass.
1⅔ shots Don Julio Añejo tequila
1 shot Choya Umeshu-Dento
⅔ shot St Raphael Ambre vermouth
⅓ shot Pedro Ximénez sherry
2 dashes Jerry Thomas bitters
4 sprigs Lemon thyme
Alcohol per serving: 11.8g

Elixir Margarita (classic)

Glass: Tumbler
Garnish: Black olive tapenade, copil cactus fruit, lime segments
Method: SHAKE all ingredients with ice and fine strain into ice-filled glass.
1⅛ shot Don Julio Añejo tequila
½ shot El Capricho Elixir de Agave Reposado
½ shot Copil cactus liqueur
½ shot Agave nectar
¾ shot Freshly squeezed lime juice
1 dash Mister Frothee (cocktail foam)
Himalayan salt
Alcohol per serving: 9.7g

Torsten presented two visually stunning drinks – the first, called Temptation, an aromatic and delicate but complex martini-style cocktail poured over a homemade ice sphere transported from Germany. "Everything in the drink should complement the tequila," he said. "Thyme, cloves, cinnamon, orange peel, plum, raisin, grapefruit are all a perfect match for the heritage of the tequila. It creates a nice, balanced, adult cocktail."

His Elixir Margarita was a bold and confident manifestation of all things agave, the elixir enhancing the flavour – "my personal twist on a classic Margarita and a Tommy's Margarita", he said.

Amanda Wan
Malaysia

Unnamed (signature)
Glass: Flute
Garnish: Basil leaf
Method: SHAKE first five ingredients, fine strain into flute, top with champagne, 'lifting' with barspoon.
1½ shots Zacapa 23 rum
6 cubes Fresh mango
1 shot Mango purée
4 Basil leaves
1 Cinnamon stick
Champagne to top
Alcohol per serving: 7.1g

Mai Tai (classic)
Glass: Tumbler
Garnish: Orange zest twist
Method: SHAKE all ingredients with ice and strain into ice-filled glass.
1 shot Zacapa 23 rum
⅔ shot Orange Curaçao liqueur
½ shot Pampero Blanco rum
¼ shot Orgeat (almond) syrup
1 splash Freshly squeezed lime juice
Alcohol per serving: 8.9g

Sporting Zacapa 23 rum sleeve garters, made from the bottle's signature palm leaf surround, Amanda designed two cocktails to showcase the rum's flavour in contrasting ways, demonstrating a delicate and precise technique in each. For her signature cocktail, faced with 'less fragrant' mangoes than she could get in the Far East, she decided to cook down some fresh mango with brown sugar and lemon juice and combine it with mango purée in order to replicate the flavour intensity.

Felipe Navarro
Colombia

Refreshing Cucumber (signature)
Glass: Highball
Garnish: Cucumber
Method: SHAKE all ingredients with ice and strain into ice-filled glass.
1⅔ shots Tanqueray No.TEN gin
⅓ shot Bénédictine D.O.M. liqueur
⅓ shot Triple Sec liqueur
⅓ shot Freshly squeezed lime juice
Alcohol per serving: 12.5g

Tom Collins (classic)
Glass: Highball
Garnish: Lime slice and maraschino cherry
Method: BUILD first 6 ingredients in glass, fill with ice and top with soda.
1½ shots Tanqueray No.TEN gin
½ shot Sugar syrup
1 dash Angostura aromatic bitters
Juice of half a lime
⅓ shot Triple Sec liqueur
⅓ shot Freshly suqeezed lime juice
Soda water
Alcohol per serving: 10.4g

Felipe brought an efficient and no-nonsense approach to the bar Balthazar, opting for two refreshing tasting drinks which he said were perfect for a sunny Colombian day.

Ilias Marinakis
Greece

Monroy (signature)
Glass: Brandy Snifter
Garnish: Shiso leaves, pink grapefruit twist and discard
Method: DRY SHAKE then strain into glass
2 shots Tanqueray No.TEN gin infused with shiso leaves.
½ shot Rooibos tea
½ shot Freshly squeezed lime juice
⅓ shot Honey
2 dashes Grapefruit bitters
Alcohol per serving: 11.2g

Bramble (classic)
Glass: Tumbler/Old Fashioned
Garnish: Lemon zest twist
Method: SHAKE first three ingredients and strain into crushed ice filled glass, drizzle crème de mûre on top.
1⅔ shot Tanqueray No.TEN gin
1 shot Freshly squeezed lemon juice
½ shot Sugar syrup
Crème de mûre liqueur
Alcohol per serving: 10.0g

A studied, serious and methodical approach saw Ilias use almost half his allotted time preparing his first drink – and saw judge Gaz Regan reach for the clock in concern.

Nonetheless, his charisma quickly returned and he came up with a beautifully presented Monroy cocktail, named after Marilyn Monroe, while his shiso infusion seemed to really accentuate the camomile flavours of Tanqueray No.TEN gin , with the aromas captured in the snifter.

Takumi Watanabe
Japan

Botanical Garden (signature)
Glass: Martini
Garnish: Sudachi (Japanese lime) slice on surface; lemon zest 'butterfly' on the rim
Method: SHAKE all ingredients with ice and fine strain into chilled cocktail glass.
1 shot Tanqueray No.TEN gin
⅔ shot Green tea
½ shot Fresh Sudachi (Japanese lime) juice
¼ shot Sugar syrup
Alcohol per serving: 5.6g

Aviation (classic)
Glass: Martini
Garnish: Lemon zest spritzed
Method: Dry STIR gin on its own, add other ingredients, SHAKE with ice and fine strain into chilled glass.
1½ shot Tanqueray No.TEN gin
½ shot Maraschino liqueur
⅛ shot Crème de violette liqueur
⅓ shot Freshly squeezed lemon juice
Alcohol per serving: 10.6g

Sporting a Tanqueray No. TEN gin badge, there was no questioning what spirit Takumi's Cocktail Mastery challenge would centre on. His signature Botanical Garden was designed to showcase the gin's fresh botanicals, with the sudachi reflecting the coriander used in Tanqueray, and a typically intricate Japanese-style 'butterfly' garnish.

For his Aviation, Takumi first stirred the gin neat and with no ice, in order to better release its aromatic qualities. Paying close attention to the balance of the cocktail, he tasted the crème de violette liqueur, which he said was particularly strong, before and after adding maraschino and lemon juice. Did it work? Gaz Regan said: "That's the best Aviation I've ever tasted."

Thomas Huhn
Switzerland

King's Cocktail (signature)
Glass: Silver martini
Garnish: Lemon spritzed then discarded
Method: SHAKE all ingredients with ice and fine strain into chilled glass.
2 shots Don Julio Blanco tequila
⅔ shot Sweet vermouth
⅓ shot Avocado honey
1 dash Orange bitters
Alcohol per serving: 10.7g

Margarita (classic)
Glass: Martini
Garnish: Half salt rim and lime wedge
Method: SHAKE all ingredients with ice and fine strain into chilled glass.
2 shots Don Julio Blanco tequila
⅔ shot Triple Sec liqueur
⅔ shot Freshly squeezed lime juice
Alcohol per serving: 12.7g

Thomas's silver martini glass added an extra surprise element to his signature King's Cocktail, accentuating the temperature of the drink and radiating coldness. Mexican avocado honey, found by chance in his local supermarket, helped create a silkily viscous drink.

Thomas chose Don Julio Blanco tequila for both his drinks: "When I work with tequila in cocktails, I most often use blanco: I think it's the most interesting."

Angus Zou
Taiwan

Martini Reviver (signature)
Glass: Chinese teacup
Garnish: Greek olives on fresh bread with balsamic reduction; barley tea chaser
Method: Toast sun-dried French bread, then pour vodka through into mixing glass; add Green Chartreuse, STIR with ice and strain into cup.
2 shots Ketel One vodka
2 dashes Green Chartreuse liqueur
French bread
Barley tea
Alcohol per serving: 7.9g

Cosmopolitan (classic)
Glass: Martini
Garnish: Lemon zest garnish
Method: SHAKE all ingredients with ice and fine strain into chilled glass.
1½ shots Ketel One vodka
¾ shot Triple Sec liqueur
⅔ shot Freshly squeezed lime juice
½ shot Cranberry juice
Alcohol per serving: 10.7g

Despite some eye-catching theatre, Angus created an admirably simple signature cocktail. His Martini Reviver was imbued with a toasted nose and a delicate yeasty flavour – both elements that built on the flavour characteristics of Ketel One vodka, in a move he said was his tribute to the 300-year heritage of the brand.

For his Cosmopolitan he decided to refrain from flaming his garnish – opting for lemon rather than orange, he simply spritzed it over the surface before discarding, so as not to tarnish the clean taste of Ketel One vodka.

Rina Fermin
Venezuela

Passion de Primavera (signature)
Glass: Flute
Garnish: Fresh cherry
Method: MUDDLE dry ingredients, add tequila and SHAKE with ice, fine strain and top with soda.
1½ shot Don Julio Reposado tequila
2 Dates
3 Fresh cherries
5 Blueberries
6-7 grains Guinea pepper
1 pinch Venezuelan cocoa powder
1 soupspoon Sugar
Soda Water
Alcohol per serving: 6.7g

Caipiroska (classic)
Glass: Rocks
Garnish: Lime zest, and serve with a small wooden spoon
Method: MUDDLE lime then BUILD over crushed ice.
1½ shots Cîroc vodka
2 teaspoons White sugar
½ shot Freshly squeezed lime juice
2 slices Root ginger
Alcohol per serving: 7.1g

Rina measures the success of her signature drink on a difficult customer – with the Passion de Primavera (Springtime Passion) she says she finally had a happy guest on her hands. "When a customer says they like something but never order it again, you know they are lying," she says. "It's a great sign when they order the same thing again."

Rina specially modified the recipe for World Class, substituting fresh cherries for jams. She served her Caipiroska with a small wooden spoon, which judge Gary Regan liked the look of so much, he put it aside to take home.

Timo Janse
Netherlands

TEN to Fly (signature)
Glass: Martini
Garnish: Fig slice
Method: SHAKE all ingredients with ice and fine strain into chilled glass.
2⅛ shots Tanqueray No.TEN gin
½ shot Poire William liqueur
⅓ shot Freshly squeezed lemon juice
⅛ shot Fig syrup
Alcohol per serving: 13.4g

Pegu Club (classic)
Glass: Martini
Garnish: Spent lime (after squeeze)
Method: SHAKE all ingredients with ice and fine strain into chilled glass.
2 shots Tanqueray No.TEN gin
½ shot Triple Sec liqueur
½ shot Freshly squeezed lime juice
2 dashes Angostura aromatic bitters
2 dashes Orange bitters
Alcohol per serving: 14.6g

Timo modelled his TEN to Fly on an Aviation cocktail, but said he was being especially cautious with the flavours so as not to overwhelm the drink. "What spoils this drink is if you use too much lemon, so I use the fig syrup to balance it. I want it to be delicate with not too much texture –and I hope you find the quality of the base product shows through."

For his classic drink, a Pegu Club cocktail, he was keen that the flavour and colour of his bitters were not lost in the shaker, so he achieves a swirl of colour and an intensity of flavour by simply dripping them into the finished drink as part of the garnish.

Max La Rocca
Ireland

Striding Man (signature)
Glass: Old Fashioned/Tumbler
Garnish: Rim glass with fresh ginger then drop in glass, cinnamon powder
Method: MUDDLE ginger, add other ingredients and use a handheld cappuccino frother, then shake with ice and strain into ice-filled glass.
2 shots Johnnie Walker Gold Label Blended Scotch Whisky
⅔ shot Cinnamon syrup 1:1
3 slices Root ginger
½ shot Freshly squeezed lemon juice
½ fresh Egg white
Alcohol per serving: 9.5g

Bobby Burns (classic)
Glass: Coupette
Garnish: Lemon zest twist
Method: Add ingredients with ice and use THROWING method, fine strain into chilled glass.
1 ⅔ shot Johnnie Walker Gold Label Blended Scotch whisky
⅔ shot Sweet vermouth
1 dash Bénédictine D.O.M. liqueur
Alcohol per serving: 9.5g

Max departed from more familiar methods of mixing cocktails, first using a handheld cappuccino frother to 'dry shake' his sour mix in his signature drink; and choosing to throw his classic drink.

"I was fed up with regular whisky sours, was playing with Johnnie Walker Blended Scotch whisky – and I fell in love," says Max of his Striding Man cocktail – a drink of great complexity with a long, long finish.

His said throwing his version of a Bobby Burns produced an intensely silky mouth feel. "It produces smooth bubbles in the drink for your lips and your palate – combining the effect of aeration from shaking and dilution from stirring."

Heinz Kaiser
Austria

Lagrimas de Oro (Golden Tears) [signature]
Glass: Old fashioned wine glass/Martini
Garnish: Spritzed with orange and lemon zest, then orange zest left in the glass.
Method: STIR ingredients with ice then strain into glass smoked with lit cinnamon stick.
2 shots Zacapa 23 rum
⅔ shot Rose's lime cordial
⅓ shot Maraschino liqueur
⅛ shot Grand Marnier liqueur
2 dashes Orange bitters
Alcohol per serving: 11.5g

Zacapa Zazerac (classic)
Glass: Old-Fashioned
Garnish: None
Method: Fill Old Fashioned with crushed ice and RINSE with absinthe and Champagne – all to be discarded. STIR ingredients in a mixing glass without ice to dissolve sugar; stir a second time with ice; serve over a single, large ice cube.
2 shots Zacapa 23 rum
1½ spoons Brown sugar
3-4 dashes Peychaud's aromatic bitters
3 drops Old Fashioned Bitters
⅛ shot Absinthe
Champagne
Alcohol per serving: 12.0g

Heinz's signature cocktail was a twist on a Hemingway cocktail. "I like the drink, and I love the rum, but this will be a completely different drink," he promised. Indeed it was, highlighted by his use of a smoking cinnamon stick, which Heinz used to infuse his glass before pouring the drink into it.

For his take on a Sazerac, involved rinsing the glass with absinthe and champagne over crushed ice, before discarding the mixture. But he insisted it was not actually an expensive drink as bars tend to have champagne open – and said not much champagne was actually required.

José Luis León Martínez
Mexico

Julio el Chapulin (signature)
Glass: Flute
Garnish: Chopped-up Chapulin insect rim (Chapulin insects – cooked in a casserole then fried)
Method: SHAKE all ingredients with ice and fine strain into chilled glass.
2 shots Don Julio Blanco tequila
½ shot Sugar syrup
2 oz Xoconostle fruit (baked with sugar)
5-6 fresh Basil leaves
Alcohol per serving: 9.5g

Pear Caipiroska (classic)
Glass: Tumbler/Old Fashioned
Garnish: Lemon and baked pear slices
Method: MUDDLE lemon and sugar; add other ingredients then SHAKE with ice. Strain over crushed ice.
2 shots Cîroc vodka
2 shots Homemade pear syrup
1 teaspoon White sugar
½ fresh Lemon chopped
Alcohol per serving: 9.5g

Promising some traditional Mexican ingredients, José Luis didn't disappoint. For his signature drink, not only did he use the Xochonostle fruit, he also opened a large bag full of Chapulin insects –pre-cooked and fried – that he chopped up to create an unusual rim for his flute. The insects' strangely citrusy flavours was a remarkable foil for the blanco tequila.

Richard Gonzalez
Dominican Republic

Don Julio Spectrum (signature)
Glass: Cosmopolitan (Martini without stem)
Garnish: 3:1 sugar/cardamom powder rim. Blue Curaçao and grenadine run down inside of both sides of glass
Method: DRY BLEND lime, syrup, mango and coriander; then shake with tequila, fine strain into chilled cocktail glass and drizzle blue curaçao and grenadine into drink.
2 shots Don Julio Añejo tequila
1 shot Freshly squeezed lime juice
1¼ shots Sugar syrup
1½ shots Mango purée
6 leaves Coriander
½ shot Raspberry liqueur
½ shot Crème de mûre liqueur
1 dash Blue Curaçao liqueur
1 dash Grenadine syrup
Alcohol per serving: 10.8g

Tamarind Margarita (classic)
Glass: Martini
Garnish: Salt rim
Method: SHAKE ingredients with ice and fine strain into chilled cocktail glass.
2 shots Don Julio Añejo tequila
1 shot Triple Sec liqueur
1¼ shot Freshly squeezed lime juice
1¼ shot Tamarind concentrate
Alcohol per serving: 13.7g

"One of the most interesting tidbits I learned about this tequila is that according to Don Julio's own form of quality control, newly made glass bottles are rinsed not with water but with tequila," says Richard, impressing judge Gaz Regan with a new dinner party fact. It was a prelude to two spectacularly colourful and interesting drinks, offering a taste of the Dominican Republic through his signature Don Julio Spectrum and his twist on a Margarita.

Arnaldo Hernandez
Puerto Rico

Latin Flavour (signature)
Glass: Martini
Garnish: Rose petals, blackberry, pineapple and red berries, decorated with sugar paint
Method: Blend blackberries, blueberries, lemon juice and syrup; then shake with other ingredients and double strain into chilled glass.
1 shot Zacapa 23 rum
¼ shot Passion fruit and honey vodka infusion
¼ shot Ginger, celery root, guava and vanilla bean vodka infusion
¼ shot Mamoncillo, anise and cinnamon vodka infusion
1½ shots Sugar syrup
1 shot Freshly squeezed lemon juice
6-7 Blackberries
6-7 Blueberries
Alcohol per serving: 8.3g

Ultimate Caipirissima (classic)
Glass: Old Fashioned
Garnish: Fresh blackberry, lemon and lime small chunks
Method: MUDDLE, SHAKE and strain over crushed ice.
2 shots Zacapa 23 rum
2 barspoons Whit sugar
1 wedge Lemon
1 wedge Lime
¼ shot Freshly squeezed lemon juice
¼ shot Freshly squeezed lime juice
1 wedge Orange
Alcohol per serving: 9.5g

Puerto Rico's finest came up with two contrasting cocktails: his classic, a simple affair, where Zacapa 23 rum was complemented by citrus juices; his signature, a multi-flavoured blend of three homemade infusions (each containing several fruits, roots, herbs and spices) and fresh fruit, appropriately called the Latin Flavour.

Noach Van Damme
Belgium

Aqua Regia (King's Water) [signature]
Glass: Old-Fashioned/Tumbler
Garnish: Served on an i-Phone
Method: Shaken then strained onto cubed ice, topped with layer of frothed milk.
1⅓ shots Johnnie Walker Gold Label Blended Scotch Whisky
1 shot Pedro Ximénez sherry
⅔ shot Speculaaslikeur
2 dashes Jerry Thomas bitters
2 dashes Old Time aromatic bitters
1 sheet Gold leaf
Frothed milk
Alcohol per serving: 11.1g

Blood & Sand (classic)
Glass: Martini
Garnish: Orange-zested rim, spritzed then discarded
Method: SHAKE and fine strain into chilled glass.
1 shot Johnnie Walker Gold Label Blended Scotch Whisky
⅔ shot Cherry brandy liqueur
⅔ shot Sweet vermouth
1 shot Fresh orange juice
Alcohol per serving: 7.8g

Noach combined a joke-laden patter with informed historical detail about the products he used in his drinks.

He made no bones about his first drink, efficiently shaking up a Blood and Sand, creating a drink that judge, Gaz Regan said really complemented the Johnnie Walker Gold Label Blended Scotch Whisky.

But Noach kept his powder dry for his signature drink – a sweet and spicy, well-balanced cocktail that was brought to life by the addition of a sheet of gold leaf in the shaker. The visual effect was doubled by the milk foam layer that topped the drink, and an iPhone 'coaster' running an app that lit up the drink like lightning.

WINNER
Torsten Spuhn
Germany

Cocktails and Canapés

A challenge designed to test our bartenders' ability to harmonise their alcoholic creativity with food – and with increasing numbers of bars and restaurants matching food not just with wine but with cocktails, a real and meaningful challenge too.

Competitors were first given an initial tasting of six previously-unseen and untasted dishes, from sashimi through to sweet dessert, before choosing two to complement with Diageo Reserve spirits and a limited selection of liqueurs, juices, fruits and spices in drinks of their own creation.

With just 40 minutes to hone their two cocktails, they then faced judge Professor Alfredo Sorias – perhaps the most serious, meticulous customer they have ever encountered – and presented their two pairings to him in a further ten minutes, with points awarded for presentation, communication of the base spirit and most importantly their ability to pair those flavours with the culinary creations of world-renowned Nobu Matsuhisa.

On the menu, courtesy of executive chef Jerome Lorvellec and executive sushi chef Katsu Hanamure, were the following choices:

1. **White Fish Tiradito**
   Thin slices of sea bass with a citrusy sauce and rocoto chilli paste

2. **Yellowtail Jalapeno**
   Yellowtail sashimi with a slice of jalapeno, garlic purée, coriander and yuzu soy sauce

3. **Salmon Karashi Su Miso**
   Seared salmon with a sweet and mild Japanese mustard sauce

4. **Beef New Style**
   Thinly sliced of beef with garlic puree, ginger, chives and yuzu soy sauce, seared with hot oil

5. **Chicken Anticucho**
   Chicken skewers with a spicy sauce made from two types of chili

6. **Whisky Cappuccino**
   Layers of coffee brûlée, cocoa crunch, iced milk and cream, topped with Suntory whisky foam

> **1 Shot = 15ml / ½ ounce**

Rafael Pizanti
Brazil

Special TEN gin
Glass: Sling
Garnish: Slice of grapefruit and a slice of ginger
Method: MUDDLE, shake and strain into ice-filled glass. Top with ginger ale.
2⅓ shots Tanqueray No. TEN gin
1⅔ shots Fresh grapefruit juice
⅓ shot Sugar syrup
2 drops Rose water
1 slice Root ginger
Top up with Ginger ale
Alcohol per serving: 7.5g

Rafael's first drink was a lengthy sling, full of sharp citrus and Asian spices. His delivery was quiet and thoughtful as he muddled a generous slice of ginger with rose water and sugar syrup to balance the spicy Japanese flavours of the chicken canapé.

Sweet Cucumber
Glass: Old Fashioned
Garnish: Cucumber slice, lemon slice and mint sprig
Method: MUDDLE, shake and strain into ice-filled glass.
2 shots Ketel One vodka
⅓ shot Freshly squeezed lemon juice
½ inch Cucumber
1 spoon Sugar
Alcohol per serving: 9.5g

The Sweet Cucumber saw Rafael take a simple approach to pairing with the tiradito, producing a clean, fresh flavour, served short and on the rocks.

Felipe Navarro
Columbia

TEN gin Refresh
Glass: Old Fashioned
Garnish: Cucumber slice
Method: SHAKE and strain into ice-filled glass.
1⅓ shots Tanqueray No. TEN gin
1⅔ shots Cucumber juice
1 dash Freshly squeezed lemon juice
⅓ shot Sugar syrup
Alcohol per serving: 7.5g

Felipe chose to pair his first creation with the mustardy, spicy flavours of Matsuhisa's salmon dish. The TEN gin Refresh, used freshly juiced cucumber to lighten and emphasise the herbal and spiced notes of the Tanqueray No. TEN gin.

Julio Tropical
Glass: Old Fashioned
Garnish: Mint leaves
Method: SHAKE all ingredients with ice and fine strain into ice-filled glass.
1⅔ shots Don Julio Blanco tequila
1⅔ shots Fresh orange juice
⅓ shot Sugar syrup
8 fresh Mint leaves
Alcohol per serving: 6.3g

Felipe's second cocktail was intended to match Matsuhisa's rich modern beef dish. Fresh local mint was shaken with equal parts Don Julio Blanco tequila and freshly-squeezed orange juice – plus a few dashes of sugar syrup to balance and a bruised mint leaf garnish.

Maxime Hoerth
France

Matsuhisa's Special
Glass: Martini
Garnish: Twist of lime and a lemongrass-brushed rim
Method: Muddle then shake and fine strain into chilled glass.
2 shots Tanqueray No. TEN gin
1⅓ shots Pressed apple juice
1 shot Elderflower cordial
⅔ shot Freshly squeezed lime juice
3-4 fresh Ginger pieces
Alcohol per serving: 9.4g

Maxime created a drink with a real ginger kick to complement the tiradito.

No Regrets
Glass: Old Fashioned
Garnish: Talisker spray
Method: MUDDLE then SHAKE and strain into ice-filled glass.
1⅔ shots Talisker Single Malt Scotch Whisky
⅔ shot Rose syrup
4 drops Angostura aromatic bitters
5 fresh Raspberries
Alcohol per serving: 7.9g

Looking to pair the coffee flavours of the challenge's Whisky Cappuccino dessert dish, Maxime reached for the spicier notes of the Island whisky, with a generous spray of the peated whisky to really accentuate the drink's nose.

Max La Rocca
Ireland

Basil Bay
Glass: Martini
Garnish: Basil leaf float
Method: MUDDLE pineapple; add other ingredients, SHAKE and fine strain into a chilled glass.
1⅔ shots Tanqueray No. TEN gin
⅔ shot Freshly squeezed lemon juice
⅔ shot Sugar syrup
2 fresh Pineapple chunks
5 fresh Basil leaves
Alcohol per serving: 7.5g

Max used pineapple to create sweetness and basil to act as a palate cleanser that did not overwhelm the delicacy of the sea bass. He chose Tanqueray No. TEN gin because of its grapefruit, lemon notes and spicy botanicals, to match the citrus and spice of the dish's sauce.

Smoking Sensation
Glass: Old Fashioned
Garnish: Orange zest
Method: EMULSIFY egg white with cappuccino frother, then shake and strain.
1 shot Talisker Single Malt Scotch Whisky
⅓ shot Coffee liqueur
⅓ shot Freshly squeezed lemon juice
½ shot Sugar syrup
½ shot Egg white
Alcohol per serving: 6.5g
Max wanted the smokiness of the Talisker to cut through the sweetness of the Whisky Cappuccino.

Tomas Dundulis
Dubai

Spicy Ocean
Glass: Martini
Garnish: Chilli slice
Method: MUDDLE, shake and fine strain into chilled glass.
1⅓ shots Cîroc vodka
⅙ shot Dry vermouth
⅔ shot Lychee juice
⅙ shot Sugar syrup
⅛ shot Egg white
2 fresh Chilli pieces
3 fresh Peeled cucumber slices
4 fresh Lemongrass pieces
Alcohol per serving: 6.6g

Tomas made a point of explaining every thought behind his drinks. His Spicy Ocean was paired with yellow tail, the chilli echoing the fish's jalapeño garnish, creating a light and elegant drink with a fresh, clean kick from the Cîroc vodka.

Violet Flora
Glass: Martini
Garnish: Basil leaf
Method: Muddle, shake and fine strain into chilled glass,
1⅙ shots Tanqueray No. TEN gin
⅙ shot Crème de Violette
⅓ shot Water
⅙ shot Sugar syrup
4 fresh White grapes
4 fresh Basil leaves
2 twists Lime zest
⅙ shots Freshly squeezed lime juice
Alcohol per serving: 6.9g

Sea bass was paired with a drink boasting strong herbal notes, a pleasingly bright colour and citrus flavours that made the Tanqueray No. TEN gin shine through.

Noach Van Damme
Belgium

La Vie En Rose
Glass: Martini
Garnish: None
Method: DRY SHAKE egg white, then shake with ice and fine strain into chilled glass.
2⅔ shots Ketel One vodka
½ shot Sugar syrup (1:1)
½ shot Rose syrup
⅚ shot Freshly squeezed lemon juice
⅓ shot Egg white
1 slice Chilli
Alcohol per serving: 12.6g

A delicate chilli kick to this dish, designed to pair with sea bass, with rose neatly on the nose and the vodka coming through on the finish.

Voulez-Vous Couchez?
Glass: Old Fashioned
Garnish: Flamed cinnamon
Method: STIR all ingredients with ice and strain into ice-filled glass.
1⅔ shot Talisker Single Malt Scotch Whisky
⅓ shot Coffee liqueur
⅓ shot Cinnamon syrup
2 dashes Angostura aromatics bitters
Alcohol per serving: 10.8g

This was a bittersweet drink that matched the nuances of the Whisky Cappuccino dessert.

Takumi Watanabe
Japan

Invitation
Glass: Martini
Garnish: Cucumber peel and lemon zest (discarded)
Method: MUDDLE then shake and fine strain into chilled glass.
1 shot Tanqueray No. TEN gin
1⅓ shots Fresh grapefruit juice
⅙ shot Lime liqueur
⅙ shot Sugar syrup
4 slices Cucumber
Alcohol per serving: 6.0g

Flawlessly efficient preparation and a two-step translation process (Japanese to English, English to Spanish) saw Takumi match sea bass with a seemingly simple blend of sweet and sour that used the natural citrus and spice notes of the Tanqueray No. TEN gin and a sweet cucumber nose, resulting in a refreshing, floral taste and a lengthy finish.

Superior
Glass: Martini
Garnish: Tomato, with balsamic vinegar and sugar
Method: SHAKE all ingredients with ice and fine strain into chilled glass.
1 shot Zacapa 23 rum
⅔ shot Tomato juice
⅔ shot Cranberry juice
⅓ shot Freshly squeezed lemon juice
1 spoon Fresh ginger juice
Alcohol per serving: 4.7g

A classic pairing of tomato with chicken, with the lemon and cranberry juices adding nuance to the tomato juice, ginger to match the kick in the food, and an intriguing contrast with the sweetness of the rum.

Rina Fermin
Venezuela

Sueño de Atanea
Glass: Martini
Garnish: Lychee with a lemongrass spear
Method: SHAKE all ingredients with ice and fine strain into chilled glass.
1½ shots Cîroc vodka
1½ shots Lychee juice
10g fresh Lemongrass
Rina used the clean, fresh taste of Cîroc vodka as a base for a sweet and spicy drink with traditional Asian flavours to complement Matsuhisa's salmon dish.
Alcohol per serving: 7.1g

Bahia Atica
Glass: Rocks
Garnish: Lime slice with celery leaf
Method: MUDDLE celery then shake and strain into ice-filled glass.
1½ shots Tanqueray No. TEN gin
Juice of half a lemon
10g sliced Celery
1 spoon Honey
1 shot Ginger ale
An unusual combination of flavours made for a match with yellow tail. Tropical in its sweetness, the celery provided a herbaceous touch.
Alcohol per serving: 8.4g

Richard Gonzalez
Dominican Republic

Port Novo Cosmo
Glass: Martini
Garnish: Lemon slice
Method: SHAKE all ingredients with ice and fine strain into a chilled glass.
1½ shots Ketel One Citroen vodka
¾ shot Triple Sec liqueur
¾ shot Crème de mûre liqueur
1 shot Port
1 shot Freshly squeezed lime juice
1½ shots Sugar syrup
Alcohol per serving: 14.6g

Ketel One Citroen vodka was used to bring out the lime notes in the chicken dish: a drink with quite a punch.

White Zacagria
Glass: Sling
Garnish: Fresh orange and pineapple
Method: MUDDLE then SHAKE all ingredients, strain and top with champagne.
2 shots Zacapa 23 rum
1 shots Triple Sec liqueur
¾ shot Ketel One Citroen vodka
1½ shots Pressed apple juice
1½ shots Pressed pineapple juice
1½ shots Fresh orange juice
5 shots Champagne
Alcohol per serving: 24.8g

Fresh fruit flavours and rum created a tropical contrast for the richness of the salmon dish, with a generous champagne top adding some sparkle and acidity.

Heinz Kaiser
Austria

Aviation
Glass: Snifter
Garnish: Single ice cube
Method: SHAKE all ingredients with ice and fine strain into chilled glass.
2 shots Tanqueray No. TEN gin
1 shots Freshly squeezed lemon juice
1½ shots Maraschino liqueur
1 shots Sugar syrup (1:1)
1 spoon Crème de violette liqueur
Alcohol per serving: 17.5g

Heinz steered away from the more obvious tropical flavour routes, pairing sea bass with a slightly sweeter, herbal version of an Aviation. He contrasted the spiciness of the dish's chilli and coriander flavours, using Tanqueray No. TEN gin to echo the coriander notes.

Tequila Sangrita
Glass: Snifter & Old Fashioned
Garnish:
Method: Pour Don Julio into snifter. SHAKE ingredients for sangrita with ice and strain into ice-filled old fashioned glass.
2 shots Don Julio Añejo tequila (served neat)
for the sangrita:
1 shot Tomato juice
1 dash Freshly squeezed lime juice
1 dash Fresh Orange juice
1 pinch Celery salt
1 dash Pepper
1 dash Worcestershire Sauce
1 pinch Cinnamon powder
1 pinch Chilli
Alcohol per serving: 7.5g

Two pairings in one here, with the drink combination designed to stand up to the flavours of the salmon. The process of tasting between the two drinks and the food really impressed judge Alberto Sorias.

Erik Lorincz
UK

Nozomi
Glass: Martini
Garnish: Lemongrass
Method: MUDDLE lemongrass then SHAKE and fine strain into chilled glass.
1½ shots Don Julio Blanco tequila
⅝ shot Freshly squeezed lime juice
1 shot Pressed pineapple juice
½ shot Agave nectar
1 inch Lemongrass
Alcohol per serving: 7.1g

Erik used the lemongrass to match the yuzu flavour of the yellow tail dish's sauce, creating a classic tequila and pineapple combination with admirable subtlety. A strong, light drink with plenty of agave on the nose and a smooth finish that prompted a rare congratulation from judge Alberto Sorias.

Love Me II
Glass: Martini
Garnish: Grated nutmeg
Method: DRY SHAKE egg yolk; add other ingredients, SHAKE with ice and fine strain into a chilled glass.
1½ shots Zacapa 23 rum
½ shot Chocolate liqueur
2 spoon Muscovado sugar
1 fresh Egg yolk
3 drops Angostura bitters
Alcohol per serving: 9.2g

Though admitting to not usually being a fan of dessert, Erik opted to pair his drink with the Whisky Cappuccino, choosing Zacapa 23 rum for its nutmeg, cinnamon and chocolate flavours.

Arnaldo Hernandez
Puerto Rico

Pink Moon
Glass: Martini
Garnish: Cucumber slice
Method: MUDDLE then shake with ice and fine strain into chilled glass.
1 shot Ketel One vodka
½ shot Triple Sec liqueur
½ shot Rose syrup
Juice of half a pink grapefruit
1 piece Root ginger
2 pieces Cucumber
1 dash Peach bitters
Alcohol per serving: 7.1g

A massively experienced competitor, Arnaldo's explanation of his intent was excellent and perfectly paced, and referring to Professor Sorias as "Maestro" surely didn't hurt... A 'generous' shot of Ketel One vodka with this curious combination of flavours yielded a complex yet refreshing tasting drink, strong enough to stand up to the richness and spice of the salmon.

Let's Do This
Glass: Flute
Garnish: Grated nutmeg
Method: SHAKE all ingredients with ice and fine strain into a chilled flute.
1½ shots Zacapa 23 rum
1 shot Chocolate liqueur
2 shots Coconut cream
½ shot Sugar syrup
1 pinch Grated nutmeg
Orange zest twist
Alcohol per serving: 9.1g

Another pairing for the Whisky Cappuccino, Arnaldo's drink had bags of chocolate, with nutmeg, orange and chocolate emphasising similar notes in the Zacapa 23 rum.`

Adam Brewer
Australia

Manifesto of Luxury
Glass: Martini
Garnish: Grapefruit twist
Method: STIR all ingredients with ice and strain into chilled glass.
1⅔ shots Tanqueray No. TEN gin
⅓ shot Ketel One Citroen vodka
⅓ shot Fino dry sherry
1 dash White chocolate liqueur
Alcohol per serving: 11.7g

Bringing real energy to the room, Adam's presentation was clear, knowledgeable and fun, and he really probed Matsuhisa's chefs in the preliminary tasting period – more so than any other competitor during the week – eager to understand every base herb, spice and process. His first drink was a twist on a Vesper, switching in the Tanqueray No. TEN gin and a Ketel One Citroen vodka for the citrus notes, with a little dry sherry to balance and a touch of chocolate to sweeten and increase the drink's complexity: perfect for sea bass.

Helen of Troy
Glass: Balloon
Garnish: Orange zest twist
Method: STIR all ingredients with ice and fine strain into glass.
1 ⅓ shots Talisker Single Malt Scotch whisky
⅔ shot Tawny port
1 dash Bénédictine D.O.M. liqueur
Alcohol per serving: 9.2g

The whisky in Adam's second drink paired well with the sesame oil in the beef dish, bringing not just smoke but dry cacao, and Benedictine for some subtle spice, and to complement the dish's honey characteristics.

Ilias Marinakis
Greece

Don Julio's Twisted Bass
Glass: Old Fashioned
Garnish: Grapefruit zest twist and three basil leaves
Method: SHAKE all ingredients with ice and fine strain into ice-filled glass.
2 shots Don Julio Reposado tequila
⅔ shot Fresh grapefruit juice
⅓ shot Agave nectar
5 slices Root ginger
6 fresh Basil leaves
Alcohol per serving: 9.0g

Ilias was looking to extend the floral and spice notes of Matsuhisa's dishes, pairing sea bass with a well-structured and herbaceous take on a Tommy's Margarita.

Balsamic Dots
Glass: Old Fashioned
Garnish: Orange zest
Method: STIR all ingredients with ice and strain into ice-filled glass.
2 shots Talisker Single Malt Scotch whisky
⅙ shot Sweet vermouth
⅙ shot Honey
1 dash Balsamic vinegar
Alcohol per serving: 11.1g

Ilias created a very masculine, rich drink, subtly blending smokiness with hints of orange for a long finish that paired well with Matsuhisa's beef dish.

Amanda Wan
Malaysia

Sea Fairy
Glass: Collins
Garnish: Pink grapefruit wedge
Method: MUDDLE pineapple in grapefruit juice, shake and fine strain into ice-filled glass. Top with soda.
1½ shots Tanqueray No. TEN gin
1 shot Fresh pink grapefruit juice
3 cubes Fresh pineapple
Soda water
Alcohol per serving: 8.4g

Grapefruit balanced the sweetness of the pineapple, giving a citrus sharpness that was matched by the Tanqueray No. TEN gin and which worked well with the sea bass.

Friend of Phô
Glass: Martini
Garnish: Mint leaf
Method: MUDDLE olives then shake and fine strain into shilled glass.
1 ⅔ shots Ketel One Citroen vodka
1 shot Olive brine
⅓ shot Sugar syrup (1:1)
8 fresh Mint leaves
3 Olives
Alcohol per serving: 7.9g

Matsuhisa's beef sashimi reminded Amanda strongly of a Vietnamese noodle dish often served with mint, so her cocktail was made to match the sweetness and consistency of the beef's sauce.

Thomas Huhn
Switzerland

Sea Brass
Glass: Martini
Garnish: Lemon zest twist
Method: MUDDLE lemongrass, SHAKE with ice and fine strain into chilled glass.
1⅔ shots Ketel One vodka
⅔ shot Dry vermouth
½ shot Freshly squeezed lime juice
1 piece Lemongrass
Alcohol per serving: 9.1g

Thomas produced a light, dry and slightly sharp cocktail, using lime and vodka, as he does in his own venue, to add lightness and texture to the sea bass.

Ginger & Basil martini
Glass: Martini
Garnish: Slice of ginger
Method: MUDDLE ginger, press basil leaves; add other ingredients, SHAKE with ice and fine strain into chilled glass.
1 ⅔ shots Tanqueray No. TEN gin
½ shot Lime cordial
⅙ shot Freshly squeezed lime juice
⅓ shot Pressed apple juice
3 slices Root ginger
3 fresh Basil leaves
Alcohol per serving: 9.3g

A twist on a Gimlet to pair with beef, Thomas' second drink was refreshingly herbaceous with a fresh, citric finish.

Do-Hwan Eom
Korea

Time For Sushi
Glass: Martini
Garnish: Cucumber
Method: MUDDLE chilli and cucumber; add other ingredients, SHAKE with ice and fine strain into chilled glass.
1⅙ shots Tanqueray No. TEN gin
⅓ shot Freshly squeezed lemon juice
1 slice Chilli
3 slices Cucumber
½ fresh Egg white
Alcohol per serving: 6.5g

A veritable pile-up of translators bridged the gap from Korean to English, then English to Spanish for Professor Sorias. Do-Hwan's first drink was paired with sea bass: an aperitif-style cocktail, with a light combination of flavours adapted for the judge's palate, using cucumber to echo the fish's garnish.

Sun-Kissed Milk
Glass: Martini
Garnish: Orange zest
Method: SHAKE all ingredients with ice and fine strain into chilled glass.
1⅛ shot Zacapa 23 rum
⅓ shot Coffee liqueur
1 shot Freshly squeezed orange juice
½ shot milk
Alcohol per serving: 7.3g

A dessert drink which really built on the inherent sweetness of the Zacapa 23 rum, with coffee and orange notes to pair with the dessert, lengthened and softened with milk.

Torsten Spuhn
Germany

T-Punch #3
Glass: Old Fashioned
Garnish: Lime zest twist, slice of ginger and slice of lemongrass
Method: MUDDLE lemongrass and ginger, SHAKE with ice and fine strain into ice-filled glass.
1⅔ shot Zacapa 23 rum
½ shot Agave nectar
1 shot Freshly squeezed lime juice
8cm fresh Lemongrass
3 slices Root ginger
1 dash Old Time aromatic bitters
1 dash Angostura aromatic bitters
Alcohol per serving: 8.3g

The only competitor to bring his own ice to the round, Torsten created elegant, enormous spherical ice balls, which he re-trimmed to perfectly fit the rounded Old Fashioned glass. Choosing to pair his first drink with the beef canapé, he matched the Asian flavours with ginger and lemongrass, and used agave nectar as a healthier – and more complex – sweetener than sugar syrup. All in all, the rum really shone through, with a dry and fresh finish.

Chocolate Old Fashioned
Glass: Old Fashioned
Garnish: Lemon and orange zest twists
Method: STIR all ingredients and strain into ice-filled glass.
1 ⅔ shot Zacapa 23 rum
⅓ shot Chocolate liqueur
4 drops Old Time aromatic Bitters
2 drops Angostura aromatic Bitters
1 drop Peach bitters
Alcohol per serving: 10.0g

Also choosing to tackle the crème-brûlée, this was a chocolatey, Old Fashioned-style cocktail, with citrus notes dancing lightly above the richer, bitter undertones.

Angus Zou
Taiwan

Sea Sour
Glass: Martini
Garnish: Grapefruit twist and apple fan
Method: SHAKE all ingredients with ice and fine strain into chilled glass.
1½ shots Tanqueray No. TEN gin
⅝ shot Dry vermouth
⅛ shot Amaretto liqueur
1 dash Peach bitters
1⅓ shot Pressed apple juice
Alcohol per serving: 10.4g

A very controlled sweet and sour balance for the sea bass's naturally delicate flavour, leading with a floral and fruity nose and a strong Tanqueray No. TEN gin presence.

Pinarita
Glass: Old Fashioned
Garnish: Basil leaves
Method: MUDDLE, then shake and fine strain into ice-filled glass.
1⅔ shots Don Julio Blanco tequila
⅓ shot Freshly squeezed lime juice
⅓ shot Agave nectar
⅔ shot Freshly squeezed grapefruit juice
⅔ shot Pressed apple juice
1 fresh Basil leaf
1 slice Fresh pineapple
Alcohol per serving: 7.9g

Pairing his second drink with salmon, Angus gently torched the pineapple with a coating of black pepper before muddling it, creating a gentle smokiness which tied in nicely with the Don Julio tequila.

Esteban Delgado Badilla
Costa Rica

Sweet Red Water
Glass: Rocks
Garnish: Cucumber slice
Method: SHAKE all ingredients and strain into ice-filled glass.
1½ shots Tanqueray No. TEN gin
2 shots Tomato juice
Juice of half a lemon
1 spoon Caster sugar
Alcohol per serving: 8.4g

A sweetness from the Tanqueray No. TEN gin contrasted with fruity tomato juice, paired with the lightly spiced sea bass.

Fresh Don Julio Saque
Glass: Rocks
Garnish: Ginger wheel
Method: SHAKE all ingredients with ice and strain into ice-filled glass.
1½ shots Don Julio Blanco tequila
½ shots Pressed apple juice
3 spoon Sugar syrup
1 Lychee in syrup
1 slice Root ginger
Alcohol per serving: 7.1g

A traditional tropical flavour pairing for the chicken canapé, with the spice of the Don Julio Blanco tequila sitting nicely alongside the chicken.

Jordi Otero
Spain

Tigermilk
Glass: Martini
Garnish: Green chilli
Method: SHAKE ingredients with ice and fine strain into chilled glass.
2 shots Don Julio Reposado tequila
2⅔ shots Tigermilk (a mixture of lime juice, green chilli, honey, red chilli, sugar, 5ml Talisker Single Malt Scotch Whisky and 5ml Tanqueray No. TEN gin, juice of one lime, 10ml honey, ¼ green chilli)
Alcohol per serving: 10.9g

Looking slick in his white waistcoat and matching tie, and taking care to explain the structure and flavour processes of both his drinks and the food with which they were paired, Jordi first paired the coriander flavours of the tiradito with Tanqueray No. TEN gin, using the Don Julio Reposado tequila to balance the dish's chilli. It made for a bracingly sour drink with a tiny kick that earned a thoughtful and sincere "muy bien" from the professor.

Golden Mash
Glass: Snifter
Garnish: None
Method: MUDDLE, STIR without ice and strain into chilled glass.
2 shots Johnnie Walker Gold Label Blended Scotch Whisky
1 Lemon (quartered)
½ spoon Brown sugar
½ spoon Caster sugar
1 spoon Honey
Alcohol per serving: 9.5g

Using pre-chilled Johnnie Walker Gold Label Blended Scotch Whisky, Jordi avoided ice to retain the whisky's texture, stirred for the same reason, and created a sweet, complex, gently fruity cocktail with a long, soft Johnnie Walker finish, all of which matched the spiced sweetness of the chicken

Timo Janse
Netherlands

Big Tail
Glass: Snifter
Garnish: Lemon zest twist and flamed nutmeg
Method: DRY SHAKE then SHAKE with ice and fine strain into a chilled glass.
1¹⁄₆ shots Talisker Single Malt Scotch Whisky
½ shot Bénédictine D.O.M.
½ shot Sweet vermouth
½ shot Freshly squeezed lemon juice
⅚ shot Water
½ fresh Egg white
Alcohol per serving: 9.6g

Timo dubbed his first cocktail the Big Tail, designed to pair with the Yellowtail canapé. Using water as an active ingredient (complete with historical explanation) to soften and combine all the flavours, this was a softly sweet drink which echoed the dish's spicy complexity.

Flower of Relief
Glass: Sling
Garnish: Lime zest and local flower served up on the side
Method: SHAKE all ingredients with ice and strain into ice-filled glass.
1⅚ shot Tanqueray No. TEN gin
⅔ shot Dry vermouth
¼ shot Crème de violette liqueur
½ shot Elderflower cordial
½ shot Freshly squeezed lime juice
Alcohol per serving: 12.0g

Using a comparatively small pour of 35ml of the Tanqueray No. TEN gin, Timo explained his drink as the "female perspective" to the bar experience: it was made and served with flowers-galore and garnished with a side serving of one of the enormous tropical flowers from Matsuhisa's garden outside – a beautiful accompaniment to the chicken dish.

Richard Gillam
Singapore

Pan Alto
Glass: Martini
Garnish: Cucumber wheel and mint leaf
Method: STIR all ingredients with ice and strain into chilled glass.
1⅚ shots Don Julio Blanco tequila
½ shot Dry vermouth
1⅓ shots Pressed apple juice
¼ shot Agave nectar
8-10 Mint leaves
6 slices Cucumber
Alcohol per serving: 9.6g

Richard balanced the subtlety of the snapper with Don Julio Blanco tequila, balancing the intensity with dry vermouth: light, sweet and refreshing yet pleasantly complex.

Nam Thai
Glass: Sling
Garnish: Ginger wheel and chilli
Method: MUDDLE then SHAKE with ice and strain into ice-filled glass.
1⅔ shots Ketel One Citroen vodka
1⅔ shots Coconut milk
⅔ shot Agave nectar
1 piece Lemongrass
1 slice Root ginger
1 piece Chilli
Alcohol per serving: 7.9g

Richard used the beef dish's prominent ginger as a starting flavour, and opted for a Thai twist with coconut milk to soften the Ketel One vodka, creating a sweet and subtle drink that really stood out from the rest with its uniquely Asian flavours and textures.

José Luis León Martínez
Mexico

Cucumber Ketel
Glass: Martini
Garnish: Cucumber wedge
Method: MUDDLE mint; add other ingredients, SHAKE with ice and fine strain into chilled glass.
2 shots Ketel One vodka
½ shot Freshly squeezed lime juice
3 spoons Caster sugar
8 fresh Mint leaves
Alcohol per serving: 9.5g

José Luis paired his first drink with snapper. The result: a fresh drink with the lightness of cucumber, the tang of citrus and a hint of chilli on the finish to balance the food.

TEN gin Long
Glass: Sling
Garnish: Lemon zest twist
Method: SHAKE all ingredients and fie strain into ice-filled glass.
2 shots Tanqueray No. TEN gin
1 shot Lime cordial
1 shot Freshly squeezed lemon juice
4 fresh Basil leaves
3 wedges Lemon
top up with Sparkling water
Alcohol per serving: 11.2g

The light citrus and herbal notes of Tanqueray No. TEN gin perfectly softened and balanced the spiciness in the chicken canapé without interfering with its delicate flavours.

WINNER
Jordi Otero
Spain

Judge's comments: "This experience has been a very interesting one, a very serious one and a very necessary one: I think this challenge is particularly good at enriching bar culture."

Market Challenge

A test of creativity, and of thinking on your feet: armed with 40 Euros or the choice of the contents of a mystery box, the Market Challenge gave free rein to bartenders, challenged produce two cocktails in 50 minutes using produce from the local market.

They had to source ingredients, working to a budget, then prep and present the drinks to judge Dale DeGroff. Those most successful at the challenge were quick-witted and calm under pressure.

The task saw an array of exotic local ingredients emerge, from pine honey to red wine, ouzo and Greek citron fruits, as well as some more familiar fresh local fruits and vegetables.

1 Shot = 15ml / ½ ounce

Takumi Watanabe
Japan

Farm Paradise
Glass: Collins
Garnish: Basil leaf
Method: SHAKE all ingredients with ice and strain into ice-filled glass.
1¼ shots Tanqueray No. TEN gin
1 shot Fresh carrot juice
2⅓ shots Fresh orange juice
1 dash Ouzo
1 dash Orange bitters
4-5 Basil leaves
1 dash Cracked black pepper
Alcohol per serving: 7.4g

Summer Vacation
Glass: Martini
Garnish: Grated chocolate
Method: BLEND coffee and biscuit, add rum, shake and fine strain into chilled glass.
1⅓ shots Zacapa 23 rum
1⅓ shots Milked coffee
3 pieces Biscuit
Alcohol per serving: 9.4g

Rafael Pizanti
Brazil

Sweet Guava
Glass: Sling
Garnish: Lime wedge
Method: SHAKE and strain into ice-filled glass.
2⅔ shots Tanqueray No. TEN gin
1⅔ shots Guava juice
⅔ shot Jasmine tea
⅓ shot Ouzo
Alcohol per serving: 16.5g

Brazilian Gold
Glass: Shot
Garnish: Lemon slice
Method: SHAKE and fine strain into chilled glass.
2⅔ shots Johnnie Walker Gold Label Blended Scotch Whisky
1⅔ shots Blackberry juice
⅔ shot Créme de cassis liqueur
⅓ shot Freshly squeezed lemon juice
Alcohol per serving: 7.0g

Tomas Dundulis
Dubai

Mexican Roast
Glass: Martini
Garnish: Three coffee beans
Method: MUDDLE coffee beans then add other ingredients, SHAKE with ice and fine strain into chilled glass.
15 Coffee beans (roasted in caramel and tequila)
1⅔ shots Don Julio Añejo tequila
⅓ shot Agave nectar
⅓ shot Caramel syrup
1 shot Espresso
Alcohol per serving: 7.0g

Bazztilia
Glass: Martini
Garnish: Inside out basil leaf
Method: MUDDLE basil and nectarine; add other ingredients, SHAKE with ice and fine strain into chilled glass.
4 Basil leaves
¼ Nectarine
1 shots Mango juice
1⅓ shots Tanqueray No. TEN gin
½ shot Freshly squeezed lime juice
⅛ shot Egg white
⅔ shot Triple Sec liqueur and brown sugar mix (cooked)
Alcohol per serving: 7.0g

Jordi Otero
Spain

Papa's martini
Glass: Martini
Garnish: Caramelized ginger
Method: SHAKE ingredients with ice and fine strain into chilled glass.
2 shots Cardamom-infused Ketel One vodka
2⅔ shots Freshly squeezed lemon juice
⅔ shots Ginger syrup
Alcohol per serving: 7.0g

Orchard Breeze
Glass: Collins
Garnish: Apple fan
Method: SHAKE ingredients and strain into ice-filled glass.
1⅓ shots Ketel One vodka
1⅓ shots White wine
2 shots Pressed apple juice
⅔ shot Grape juice
⅔ shot Freshly squeezed lime juice
Alcohol per serving: 8.2g

Richard Gillam
Singapore

Pear of Skye
Glass: Martini
Garnish: Anise-dusted pear fan
Method: SHAKE all ingredients with ice and fine strain into chilled glass.
2 shots Talisker Single Malt Scotch Whisky
1⅔ shots Pear purée
⅔ shot fresh Vanilla syrup
1 bar spoon Cardamom
½ bar spoon Aniseed
Alcohol per serving: 10.8g

Lassis Los Altos
Glass: Sling
Garnish: Fennel flowers
Method: BLEND and strain into ice-filled glass.
2 shots Don Julio Blanco tequila
2 shots Greek style yoghurt
1 shot Honey
1 bar spoon Cumin
2 slices Fennel
½ Fresh mango
Alcohol per serving: 9.5g

Amanda Wan
Malaysia

Pico Shake
Glass: Martini
Garnish: Chocolate-dipped wafer and cinnamon stick
Method: MUDDLE banana and pineapple with syrup, add rum and liqueur, SHAKE and strain into ice-filled glass coated inside with chocolate sauce. Float cream and garnish.
2 shots Zacapa 23 rum
½ shot Cinnamon & nutmeg liqueur
1 ripe Banana
2inch Fresh pineapple chink
1 dash Sugar syrup
1 tablespoon Cream
Chocolate sauce
Alcohol per serving: 10.7g

Stroll down Glyfada
Glass: Martini
Garnish: Dehydrated orange slice
Method: MUDDLE orange peel in bottom of glass with sugar syrup, add all other ingredients and roll gently with ice, then fine strain into chilled cocktail glass.
1½ shots Tanqueray No. TEN gin
⅓ shot Citrus leaves liqueur
1 shot Jasmine tea
⅓ shot Lychee juice
1 broad Orange peel
1 dash Sugar syrup
Alcohol per serving: 9.8g

Erik Lorincz
UK

Muchacha Caliente
Glass: Highball
Garnish: Celery stick, served with green salad
Method: Pour into shaker and ROLL with ice, strain into ice-filled glass.
1½ shots Don Julio Blanco tequila
⅔ shot Freshly squeezed lime juice
½ shot Bloody Mary mix (flavoured salt, chili, pepper, fino sherry, mustard, basil, Worcestershire sauce)
3 ⅓ shots tomato juice
Alcohol per serving: 7.1g

Attica Cobbler
Glass: Goblet
Garnish: Cherries, lemon peel, redcurrants.
Method: MUDDLE cherries then add other ingredients, SHAKE with ice and strain into ice-filled glass.
1½ shots Tanqueray No. TEN gin
½ shot Fino dry sherry
⅔ shot Freshly squeezed lemon juice
1 shot Fresh pineapple juice
½ shot Sugar syrup (1:1)
4 Cherries
Alcohol per serving: 8.4g

Maxime Hoerth
France

Greek Margarita
Glass: Old Fashioned
Garnish: Lime zest twist
Method: POUR Naxos into ice-filled glass, TOP with water and leave to stand. Separately SHAKE next 3 ingredients ice. DISCARD contents of glass (naxos, water and ice) and FINE STRAIN contents of mixer into naxos-coated glass. Top with foam.
1⅔ shots Jasmine tea-infused Don Julio Blanco tequila
½ shot Naxos citron fruit juice
1 shot Freshly squeezed lime juice
1 shot Triple Sec liqueur
Foam (3 egg whites, dash sugar syrup (2:1), Eres Crefan bitters)
Alcohol per serving: 12.6g

Last Minute
Glass: Wine
Garnish: Mint sprigs
Method: MUDDLE fruits and herbs, add other ingredients, STIR with crushed ice, transfer all to wine glass.
1⅔ shots Tanqueray No. TEN gin
10 Mint leaves
¾ Nectarine
⅔ shot Freshly squeezed lime juice
1⅓ shots Peloponnese white wine
Alcohol per serving: 11.2g

Adam Brewer
Australia

The Mad Hatter
Glass: Snifter
Garnish: Lemon twist, flambéed walnuts, Jamon and bitter chocolate
Method: POUR ingredients into a warmed glass and rest the bowl on an old-fashioned glass. FLAME and carefully move the glass back to an upright position. STIR, garnish and serve.
1⅔ shots Zacapa 23 rum
⅓ shot Hazelnut syrup
2 dashes Angostura aromatic bitters
⅛ shot Pine honey
Camomile mist
Alcohol per serving: 8.6g

Red Dragon
Glass: Sling
Garnish: Cherry and lemon twist
Method: SHAKE ingredients and strain into ice-filled glass.
1⅔ shots Talisker Single Malt Scotch Whisky
⅛ shot Triple Sec liqueur
3 fresh Cherries
2 dashes Angostura aromatic bitters
1⅓ shot Watermelon juice
Alcohol per serving: 10.3g

Do-Hwan Eom
Korea

My Own Greek Salad
Glass: Martini
Garnish: Muddled ingredients in tomato
Method: MUDDLE all ingredients except gin, egg white and feta cheese.
1½ shots Tanqueray No. TEN gin
⅔ shot Freshly squeezed lemon juice
⅔ shot Olive oil
½ shot Honey
1 Egg white
Feta cheese
⅓ Cucumber
15g green salad
5g onion
4 olives
Alcohol per serving: 8.4g

Smoky rosemary
Glass: Old Fashioned
Garnish: Rosemary sprig
Method: STIR with ice and strain into ice-filled glass.
1½ shots Talisker Single Malt Scotch Whisky
⅔ shot Honey
⅔ shot Freshly squeezed lemon juice
1 sprig Rosemary
Alcohol per serving: 8.1g

Timo Janse
Netherlands

Royal
Glass: Sling
Garnish: Oregano and pear
Method: SHAKE ingredients and strain into ice-filled glass.
2 shots Tanqueray No. TEN gin
¾ shot Poire William liqueur
¾ shot Freshly squeezed lime juice
1 shot Fresh pear juice
½ shot Sugar syrup (1:1)
2 sprigs Oregano
Alcohol per serving: 13.4g

Papa Don Fig
Glass: Rocks
Garnish: Cucumber and fig slice
Method: MUDDLE cucumber, add other ingredients, stir and strain into ice-filled glass.
2 shots Don Julio Añejo tequila
¼ shot Fig jam
2 dashes Lemon bitters
2 dashes Angostura aromatic bitters
2 slices Cucumber
Alcohol per serving: 9.7g

Angus Zou
Taiwan

Poseiden
Glass: Wine
Method: SHAKE ingredients, strain into ice-filled glass.
2 shots Tanqueray No. TEN gin
1½ shots Lychee juice
⅛ shot Peach liqueur
⅓ shot Honey
1 shot White wine
Alcohol per serving: 11.4g

Summer Love
Glass: Rocks
Garnish: Grated nutmeg
Method: SHAKE ingredients and strain over crushed ice.
1⅔ shots Don Julio Blanco tequila
⅔ shot Ginger syrup
3 Cloves
1 Bay leaf
Alcohol per serving: 7.9g

Max La Rocca
Ireland

CuCu 75
Glass: Flute
Garnish: Cucumber slices
Method: MUDDLE cucumber; add other ingredients, SHAKE with ice and fine strain into chilled glass and top with champagne.
1 shot Tanqueray No. TEN gin
3 slices Fresh cucumber
⅓ shot Freshly squeezed lemon juice
⅓ shot Sugar syrup (1:1)
Alcohol per serving: 5.6g

Ring My Bell Ten Times
Glass: Martini
Garnish: Orange peel heart
Method: MUDDLE fruit and vegetables; add other ingredients, SHAKE with ice and fine strain into chilled glass.
2 shots Tanqueray No. TEN gin
⅓ Red bell pepper
½ Orange
1 fresh Peach
2 dashes Orange bitters
⅓ shot Sugar syrup (1:1)
Alcohol per serving: 11.3g

Ilias Marinakis
Greece

Worry Doll
Glass: Tiki
Garnish: Grated nutmeg and Lemon twist
Method: SHAKE with ice and strain into ice-filled glass.
2 shots Zacapa 23 rum
⅛ shot Greek floral honey
⅛ shot Sugar syrup (1:1)
2 Lychees
Thumbnail root ginger
⅔ shot Fresh grapefruit juice
1 dash Angostura aromatic bitters
3 drops Mastiha liqueur
Alcohol per serving: 10.9g

Short and Furious
Glass: Old Fashioned
Garnish: Lemon zest twist
Method: BUILD with cubed ice.
2 shots Talisker Single Malt Scotch Whisky
⅛ shot Greek floral honey
⅛ shot Blueberry marmalade
2 dash Angostura aromatic bitters
Alcohol per serving: 11.5g

Thomas Huhn
Switzerland

Heriatiki
Glass: Martini
Garnish: Mint sprig
Method: POUR ouzo into ice-filled glass, add with water and leave to stand. Separately SHAKE next other ingredients with ice. Discard contents of glass (ouzo, water and ice) and fine strain contents of mixer into ouzo-coated glass.
1⅔ shots Ketel One vodka
⅓ shot Ouzo
⅔ shot Carrot juice
⅛ shot Olive oil
⅓ shot Freshly squeezed lime juice
3 Basil leaves
Alcohol per serving: 9.5g

Greek Affair
Glass: Martini
Garnish: Lime wedge
Method: SHAKE ingredient, fine strain into chilled glass.
1 shot Talisker Single Malt Scotch Whisky
1 shot Greek red wine
½ shot Crème de cassis liqueur
1 Cinammon stick
¼ shot Raspberry jam
2 dashes Angostura aromatic bitters
⅓ shot Freshly squeezed lime juice
Alcohol per serving: 8.7g

Esteban Delgado Badilla
Costa Rica

Citrus Boble Gom
Glass: Sling
Garnish: None
Method: BLEND ingredients and pour into glass.
1½ shots Ketel One Citroen vodka
1 shot Zacapa 23 rum
1 shot Freshly squeezed lime juice
1 shot Freshly squeezed lemon juice
3 drops Lemon bitters
1 scoop Vanilla ice cream
⅓ shot Maraschino cherry
Alcohol per serving: 12.9g

Dia de Trabajo
Glass: Snifter
Garnish: None
Method: SHAKE all ingredients except beer, then fine strain into glass and top with beer.
2 shots Don Julio Blanco tequila
3 fresh Cherry tomatoes
2 grinds Black pepper
1 small Spicy chili
½ shot Freshly squeezed lime juice
Beer
Alcohol per serving: 12.2g

José Luis León Martínez
Mexico

Rico Rico
Glass: Shot
Method: SHAKE first two ingredients, fine strain and top with champagne.
1 shot Don Julio Reposado tequila
1 shot Raspberry purée
Champagne
Alcohol per serving: 7.3g

Tanqueray Flower
Glass: Martini
Garnish: Basil flower
Method: MUDDLE basil, lemon pieces and sugar; add other ingredients, SHAKE with ice and fine strain into chilled glass.
1½ shots Tanqueray No. TEN gin
8 Basil leaves
8 small Lemon pieces
2 bar spoons Sugar
1 shot Freshly squeezed lime juice
1½ shots Pear juice
Alcohol per serving: 8.4g

Torsten Spuhn
Germany

The Grey Flannel
Glass: Martini
Garnish: Pink grapefruit twist
Method: SHAKE with ice and fine strain into chilled glass.
1⅓ shots Tanqueray No. TEN gin
⅛ shot Mandarin marmalade
1⅓ shots Earl Grey tea (cold and strong)
4cm Lemongrass (diced)
Alcohol per serving: 9.3g

Apple and Celery Julep
Glass: Collins
Garnish: Sage, green apple and Lemon twist
Method: BUILD and SWIZZLE in glass with crushed ice.
1⅔ shots Ketel One vodka
1⅔ shots Pressed apple juice
8 Sage leaves
2 drops Vanilla essence
3 drops Celery bitters
Alcohol per serving: 8.9g

Richard Gonzalez
Dominican Republic

Melon Monkey
Glass: Martini
Garnish: Melon wedge and banana slice
Method: SHAKE with ice and fine strain into chilled glass.
1½ shots Zacapa 23 rum
1 shot Ketel One Citroen vodka
1 shot Ginger beer syrup
3 shots Watermelon & banana purée
Alcohol per serving: 11.8g

Jalisco white dream
Glass: Flute
Garnish: Toblerone white chocolate shavings. Choc syrup swirled glass
Method: SHAKE with ice and fine strain into chilled cocktail glass.
1½ shots Don Julio Blanco tequila
1 shot Baileys Irish cream liqueur
¾ shot Hazelnut liqueur
¼ Vanilla ice cream
1½ shots melted Toblerone white chocolate
Alcohol per serving: 11.2g

Noach Van Damme
Belgium

Potential
Glass: Flute
Garnish: Ginger slice
Method: MUDDLE ginger; add other ingredients, SHAKE with ice and fine strain into chilled glass.
1⅓ shot Don Julio Añejo tequila
1 inch Root ginger
8 Raspberries
¼ shot Honey
½ shot Freshly squeezed lime juice
Alcohol per serving: 7.5g

βBlocker
Glass: Martini
Garnish: None
Method: STIR with ice and strain into chilled glass.
1⅔ shot Zacapa 23 rum
1 shot Sweet vermouth
¼ shot Amarena cherry syrup
1 dash Angostura orange bitters
2 dashes Old Fashioned aromatic bitters
Alcohol per serving: 10.3g

Heinz Kaiser
Austria

Martinike
Glass: Martini
Garnish: Lemon zest twist
Method: MUDDLE apple, saffron and ginger, then shake and fine strain into ice-filled glass.
1⅔ shots Don Julio Reposado tequila
⅔ shot Freshly squeezed lemon juice
⅔ shot Sugar syrup (2:1)
⅛ shot Ouzo
1 shot Pressed apple juice
Saffron to taste
2-3 Apple slices
2-3 Root ginger slices
Alcohol per serving: 8.1g

Omorphia
Glass: Martini
Garnish: None
Method: MUDDLE all the solid ingredients, add all the other ingredients, shake hard and fine strain into a chilled cocktail glass.
1⅔ shots Tanqueray No. TEN gin
⅓ shot Freshly squeezed lemon juice
⅓ shot Sugar syrup (2:1)
⅙ shot Ouzo
1⅓ shots Pressed apple juice
1 Egg white
5-7 Saffron threads
3-4 slices Root ginger
3-4 slices Apple
Alcohol per serving: 10.1g

Felipe Navarro
Colombia

Francia Tropical
Glass: Collins
Garnish: Pineapple leaf
Method: SHAKE all ingredients with ice and strain into ice-filled glass.
1⅓ shot Cîroc vodka
1 shot Fresh pineapple juice
1 shot Peach juice
1 dash Freshly squeezed lime juice
Alcohol per serving: 6.3g

Amanecer de Don Julio
Glass: Snifter
Garnish: Lime wheel and carrot stick
Method: SHAKE and fine strain into snifter.
1⅔ Don Julio Blanco tequila
1 shot Fresh orange juice
1 shot Carrot juice
8 Mint leaves
Alcohol per serving: 6.3g

Arnaldo Hernandez
Puerto Rico

Running to the Market
Glass: Martini
Garnish: Honeydew melon
Method: MUDDLE the watermelon and cucumber with the sugar syrup then add all other ingredients, shake and fine strain into chilled cocktail glass. Perfume with orange bitters or roses syrup
2 shots Tequila Don Julio Añejo tequila
1 shot Triple Sec liqueur
2 pieces Watermelon
2 pieces Cucumber
½ shot Sugar syrup
½ shot Fresh pink grapefruit juice
Spray orange bitters or roses syrup
Alcohol per serving: 13.7g

Nutty Challenge
Glassware: Hurricane
Garnish: Chocolate syrup
Method: BLEND all ingredients with ice, serve in a hurricane glass decorated with chocolate syrup and chocolate dust on top.
2 shots Zacapa 23 rum
1 shot Hazelnut liqueur
2 shots Cream
2 shots Coconut cream
2 scoops Nutella spread
2 scoops Peanut butter
2 scoops Vanilla ice cream
Alcohol per serving: 12.3g

WINNER
Do-Hwan Eom
Korea

Judge's comments: "The bartenders were completely out of their comfort zone in this challenge. Even if they came into the challenge ready to recreate a few of their cocktail gems, they were faced with the reality that they would have to make substitutions. In most cases, the substitutions were unsatisfactory: this is a very difficult challenge and one that took courage.

Bartenders needed to trust themselves and their abilities and take chances, maybe make a choice to present a couple of bold flavours rather than try to layer ingredient upon ingredient in an attempt to add interest."

Ritual and Theatre

Working with just two brands – Johnnie Walker Blue Label Blended Scotch Whisky and Zacapa 23 rum – competitors were challenged to showcase a signature cocktail and a special table serve, presenting them in the most imaginative and theatrical way they could think of, using almost any tools, glassware and bar equipment possible.

It was a challenge in which the more flamboyant and extroverted contestants really shone through, with a range of presentational styles designed to highlight qualities of the spirits in unconventional and surprising ways – think interactive coasters, perfumed cards to waft, accompanying music, dry ice, fire and even national costume.

With judge Peter Dorelli presiding, he set the stakes high on the first day of the final, declaring: "I want to be flabbergasted!" He wasn't to be disappointed.

1 Shot = 15ml / ½ ounce

Timo Janse
Netherlands

Timo's first drink was called Foot, which he said "makes you ready to walk" – a play on the name of the whisky. He combined Johnnie Walker Blue Label Blended Scotch Whisky with port, a dash of peach liqueur and the citrus and oils from lime wedges.

His second drink, Nose, highlighted how to enhance a drink without mixing it with anything. Timo simply encouraged Peter to rub Zacapa 23 rum behind his ears and under his nose, and smelling peach liqueur and triple sec, before being allowed to smell and taste the rum.

José Luis León Martínez
Mexico

José Luis started out with a homely drink which he said reminded him of his mother. Called Cookies and Cream, it combined Zacapa 23 rum with condensed milk: Peter Dorelli commented that this would be a great last drink of the day – and a brilliant first drink of the next day.

José's next drink mixed Grand Marnier, mandarin liqueur and a calvados–rinsed glass with Johnnie Walker Blue Label Blended Scotch Whisky, with a choice of dried fruits. Peter opted for apricot, prune, peach and apple, which were then rehydrated with the whisky and eaten prior to sipping the chilled Scotch.

Jordi Oteri
Spain

Wearing his Mandarin Oriental uniform, Jordi set out a sake jug and bowls. He warmed jasmine tea and Zacapa 23 rum in a small tea pot over a candle, then poured it into the jug and added elderflower liqueur. With Comte cheese served as a garnish the cocktail was poured into the bowls and presented to Peter.

His second drink was a perfect serve of Johnnie Walker Blue Label Blended Scotch Whisky, with Scottish Highlands iced water rinsed around the mouth before the neat and slightly hand–warmed whisky.

Richard Gillam
Singapore

Richard began with a Guatemalan Landscape –
imagine a cross between a blazer and a hot buttered
rum – using Zapaca 23 rum and dry ice, fire,
cinnamon, butter, maple syrup, chocolate, tea and
smoked pineapple.

For his second cocktail Richard brewed Blue
Sakura Samurai Japanese tea and mixed it with
pineapple, grapefruit juice and maple syrup. This
combination served as an accompaniment to a neat
measure of Johnnie Walker Blue Label Blended
Scotch Whisky, with Scottish shortbread and local
Greek honey on the side.

Richard Gonzalez
Dominican Republic

Richard offered up an appropriately summery
cocktail, combining Zacapa 23 rum with fresh lime
juice and passion fruit syrup to create a Zacapa
Summer Passion.

Next up was a twist on a Johnnie Walker Blue
Label Blended Scotch Whisky perfect serve, with a
particularly chilling twist: his Cold as Ice serve
consisted of the whisky served in a snifter, with still
water served in a rocks glass chilled by dry ice.

Heinz Kaiser
Austria

A classically–oriented Johnnie Walker Blue Label
Blended Scotch Whisky Old Fashioned–style drink
with delicate and complementary additions of
Chambord, St. Rapheal Ambre, Honey and Fee
Brothers Old Fashioned bitters.

For his bottle serve, named Trinidad, Heinz
attempted to challenge and surprise Peter's palate
with Earl Grey tea jelly, a warm lime foam and a hot
homemade liqueur made of Zacapa 23 rum and dark
and orange chocolate. Served in small, gold–rimmed
crystal glasses and accompanied by a separate
measure of Zacapa 23 rum, each element
complemented the rum in different ways.

Erik Lorincz
UK

The signature drink provided by the UK entrant was Greek-inspired, combining Zacapa 23 rum with yoghurt liqueur, Pedro Ximenez sherry and The Bitter Truth Repeal bitters to create a flip-style drink. A complementary scent was also created by pouring dry ice over vanilla, cinnamon and cocoa, and grated Tonka beans were served as a garnish. This, Erik christened Love Me.

Erik's bottle serve was designed to highlight the different sensory perceptions experienced by serving Johnnie Walker Blue Label Blended Scotch Whisky three ways – neat in a tasting glass, on ice (over a single ice ball) and finally mixed with water. Appropriately, this was named Feminine, Masculine and Mizuwari.

Arnando Hernandez
Puerto Rico

A Charmed Island greeted judge Peter Dorelli first: a multi-coloured ice block containing fruit acting as a bottle cooler: the bottle of Zacapa 23 rum it contained infused with tamarind, pineapple, raisins and brown sugar.

The second drink involved Johnnie Walker Blue Label Blended Scotch Whisky served straight up, but with subtle additions of molasses, honey, rose petal, strawberry and chocolate with a palate-cleansing fresh ginger club soda.

Noach Van Damme
Belgium

Noach first combined Johnnie Walker Blue Label Blended Scotch Whisky with a whisky liqueur from his native Belgium and chocolate bitters for a simple but memorable cocktail, served straight up.

The second cocktail surprised guru Peter Dorelli with a technological twist: Belgian vanilla fudge, caviar and salted popcorn all complemented a glass of Zapaca 23 rum which was cleverly presented on an iPhone, displaying images of Guatemala, including the Zacapa distillery.

Tomas Dundulis
Dubai

Two contrasting serves were demonstrated by Tomas.
His Kiro Kiro mixed Zapaca 23 rum, carrot juice,
Indian cardamon, lime juice and sugar syrup. The
bright orange drink was garnished with a physalis
which perfectly matched the drink's colour.

His serve of Johnnie Walker Blue Label Blended
Scotch Whisky was complemented with a single
jasmine flower and served over ice containing another
jasmine flower frozen inside.

Rina Fermin
Venezuala

Rina brought a taste of her home country to the table
with The Creole Woman: a shot of Zacapa 23 rum
garnished with a slice of orange that was coated on
one side with papelón (lemon and raw sugar cane) and
on the other with a cocoa and guinea pepper mix – the
slice designed to be sucked before drinking the rum.

She then served Johnnie Walker Blue Label
Blended Scotch Whisky neat with honey and
cocoa-filled raspberries and a glass of water in a twist
of the perfect serve.

Takumi Watanabe
Japan

Takumi presided over a traditional Japanese tea
ceremony for Peter Dorelli, with a twist in that Zacapa
23 rum served as the 'tea', and almonds, cashew nuts,
coconut and orange peel acting as 'tea leaves'.

The bottle serve was equally impressive, with
Takumi serving a trio of Johnnie Walker Blue Label
Blended Scotch Whisky shots and manipulating
flavours by using a small smoke machine to create
cedar and oak smoke.

Do-Hwan Eom
Korea

Do-Hwan's signature drink was inspired by his Korean heritage. First sanitising his own hands, then Peter's, he laid out his ingredients on a Korean mat before creating a Zacapa 23 rum cocktail served with ginger, persimmon, cinnamon and honey. The drink was shaken and strained into Korean cups, and garnished with pinenuts and walnuts wrapped in dried persimmon.

For his second drink came a big reveal: with Scottish music playing in the background, Do-Hwan theatrically came around the front of the bar to show he was actually wearing a kilt. With this, he presented Peter with whisky served over a single ice ball

Esteban Delgado Badilla
Costa Rica

Costa Rica's finest delivered a daiquiri–like drink made from Zacapa 23 rum, fresh mango, strawberries and lime, served up in a beautiful glass.

Esteban then presented a single shot glass containing Johnnie Walker Blue Label Blended Scotch Whisky flavoured with a mix of camomile, pistachio, ginger and cinnamon, served ice cold.

Angus Zhou
Taiwan

Angus's first drink saw him flambé Zacapa 23 rum with orange, cinnamon, tobacco leaf, clove, banana and chocolate, presenting it in a small rocks glass over ice.

The table serve enabled Angus to show off his ice carving skills, creating an ice 'diamond' over which Johnnie Walker Blue Label Blended Scotch Whisky was poured.

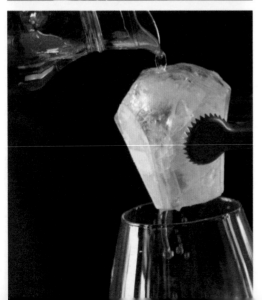

Torsten Spuhn
Germany

Time for tea with Torsten: first an Old Fashioned-style drink, containing Johnnie Walker Blue Label Blended Scotch Whisky, Earl Grey tea, pedro ximenez sherry and Creole bitters – ingredients chosen deliberately to augment flavours within the whisky, served with a garnish of black olive tapenade, organic dates and toasted salty almonds.

Torsten also used another tea in his bottle serve. Camomile tea was served separately alongside Zacapa 23 rum, the inherent sweetness of the tea and dried fruit garnish perfectly complementing the sweetness of the rum

Ilias Marinakis
Greece

Blueberries, Greek honey and vermouth were used by the home contestant to bring out elements of Johnnie Walker Blue Label Blended Scotch Whisky. This muddled then shaken drink was served in a large snifter and garnished with a few fresh blueberries.

For the second course, a traditional Greek coffee accompanied Zacapa 23 rum and was offered with Turkish Delight.

Thomas Huhn
Switzerland

Thomas's signature cocktail was a Manhattan-inspired cocktail containing Johnnie Walker Blue Label Blended Scotch Whisky, bitters, Chartreuse and sweet vermouth – served straight up in a beautiful silver martini glass.

Next came a small feast: a glass of Zacapa 23 rum with an accompaniment of Swiss nibbles including biscuits, fudge and chocolate.

Adam Brewer
Australia

Adam's signature cocktail surprised with some unconventional flavour pairings: Johnnie Walker Blue Label Blended Scotch Whisky served with quince jam, Poire William and celery bitters, all shaken together and served in a crystal snifter.

For the bottle serve challenge, Adam had gone to great lengths before the competition, filling a cask that had previously held balsamic vinegar with Zacapa 23 rum, serving the infusion direct from the barrel.

Amanda Wan
Malaysia

A theatrical approach from Amanda, with a signature cocktail combining Johnnie Walker Blue Label Blended Scotch Whisky, Chinese tea and honey. It was accompanied by aromas of chocolate from a tea pot in which dry ice had been poured over chocolate bitters – the 'smoke' was poured over tea cups containing the cocktail to create a foggy garnish that sat on the top of the drinks.

For a dessert-style table serve, Amanda presented fruitcake containing Zacapa 23 rum alongside a glass of the rum served neat.

Maxime Hoerth
France

Maxime rinsed a martini glass with Angostura bitters and Drambuie before discarding and pouring in a stirred combination of Zacapa 23 rum, Dubonnet and fig marmalade into the glass, all set off with a fresh mint leaf garnish.

Next came Johnnie Walker Blue Label Blended Scotch Whisky, poured from a crystal decanter into a large brandy snifter and served with redcurrants, raspberries, chocolate and nuts.

Max La Rocca
Ireland

Max put on a confident and impressive display by throwing a combination of Zacapa 23 rum, Heering, Aperol, orgeat and bitters before serving it in delicate glassware.

Then against the sound of Scottish music, he served Johnnie Walker Blue Label Blended Scotch Whisky with perfumed cards scented with sherry and smoke to accentuate the complexity of the whisky's nose.

Felipe Navarro
Columbia

Felipe combined Zacapa 23 rum with Columbian coffee and mango: the drink was served in layers in a martini glass, with the differing flavours to be combined in Peter Dorelli's mouth.

He then presented a classic Johnnie Walker Blue Label Blended Scotch Whisky perfect serve of neat whisky alongside a glass of ice-cold water, with the special addition of some carefully chosen accompaniments: cashews, pistachios, almonds, raspberries, strawberries and redcurrants.

Rafael Pizanti
Brazil

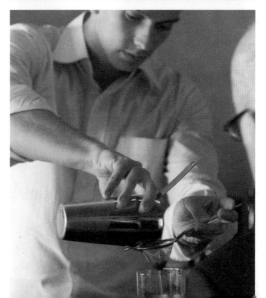

Neat Zacapa 23 rum was served by Rafael with caramelised apple, orange peel and grapefruit peel, accompanied by a Cuban cigar (to smell only, as Peter does not smoke).

The drink served at the bar to Mr Dorelli was Johnnie Walker Blue Label Blended Scotch Whisky based and was shaken and then poured in to the rocks glass.

WINNER
Max La Rocca
Ireland

Judge's comments: "All of the finalists performed extremely well, exceeding my expectations. This is a difficult challenge and requires them to show a range of skills, some artistic imagination, and to constantly seek out new ideas and concepts."

Speed and Taste

Considered a real test of day-to-day bartending, the Speed and Taste round was designed to examine how quickly and efficiently bartenders can make drinks without compromising taste. Competitors had to make judge Hidetsugu Ueno a round of six drinks in just ten minutes.

1 Shot = 15ml / ½ ounce

Cîroc Grape Caipiroska
Glass: Rocks
Garnish: Lime wedge
Method: MUDDLE fruit and sugar in base of glass.
Add other ingredients and crushed ice. Churn to mix.
Cîroc vodka
Cane sugar
Fresh cut lime
Green grapes

Tanqueray No. TEN Negroni
Glass: Rocks
Garnish: Orange slice
Method: STIR all ingredients with ice and stain into
ice-filled glass.
Tanqueray No. TEN gin
Campari
Sweet vermouth

Don Julio Margarita
Glass: Coupette
Garnish: Half salt rim
Method: SHAKE all ingredients with ice and strain
into chilled glass.
Don Julio Blanco tequila
Fresh hand-squeezed lime juice
Triple Sec liqueur

Ketel One Citroen Cosmopolitan
Glass: Martini
Garnish: Flamed orange zest twist
Method: SHAKE all ingredients with ice and strain
into chilled glass
Ketel One Citroen vodka
Triple Sec liqueur
Cranberry juice
Lime juice

Zacapa 23 Old Fashioned
Glass: Rocks
Garnish: Orange zest
Method: STIR all ingredients with ice and strain into
ice-filled glass
Zacapa 23 rum
Sugar
Aromatic bitters (choice of Angostura or orange)

Johnnie Walker Blended Scotch Whisky and soda water
Glass: Rocks
Method: POUR ingredients into ice filled glass
Johnnie Walker Gold Label Blended Scotch Whisky
Bottled soda water

WINNER
Heinz Kaiser
Austria

Judge's comments: "This challenge is important as it demonstrates what a bartender is like behind the bar on a daily basis. You must always make good drinks, but should remember your guests are waiting, and it's your job to make them feel comfortable in your bar.

"I didn't ask any questions while their routine because I wanted them to focus to their performance, but I asked them to explain their drinks while I was tasting. That's exactly the same thing they do every day behind the bar."

Classic Cocktails:
The 15 Classic Cocktails

The round demanded that each bartender make three cocktails from a list of 15 classic cocktails – each was given an envelope containing the names of the three drinks they had to make and they then had 10 minutes to set up the bar to their preference, 15 minutes to make the drinks and a further 10 minutes to answer any questions from judge Salvatore Calabrese.

The classic cocktails over the following pages are receipes supplied by Erik Lorincz, the overall winner.

1 Shot = 15ml / ½ ounce

Scotch Sour
(straight up or on the rocks – bartender's choice)
Glass: Rocks of wine glass
Garnish: Lemon zest twist (discarded). Drop the bitters on top
Method: SHAKE all ingredients with ice and fine strain into glass.
2 shots Singleton 18 or Johnnie Walker Gold or Green Label Blended Scotch Whisky
1 shot Freshly squeezed lemon juice
½ shot Sugar syrup (2:1 sugar/water)
½ shot Egg white
3 drops Angostura aromatic bitters
Alcohol per serving: 10.2g

Thomas Huhn, Switzerland
Thomas explained that he did not use any egg white in his drink because he thought this would push the whisky into background and as he was using Johnnie Walker Gold he did not want to mask its character.

Amanda Wan, Malaysia
"This is an important base for a lot of cocktail recipes", said Amanda who was one of the many competitors to dry shake her sour before re-shaking with ice."

Richard Gonzalez, Dominican Republic
Richard used 1¾ shots Johnnie Walker Gold Label Blended Scotch Whisky, 1 shot lemon juice and 1 shot Sugar syrup (1:1) and Salvatore commented of his drink, "The aromas were finely balanced between the citrus and the whisky."

Planter's Punch
(based on Trader Vic's 1947 version)
Glass: Highball
Garnish: Lime peel and mint sprig
Method: SHAKE all ingredients with ice and strain into ice-filled glass. Top with soda and gently stir.
1⅔ shots Zacapa 23 rum
⅓ shot Grenadine syrup
½ shot Sugar syrup (2:1 sugar/water)
½ shot Freshly squeezed lemon juice
½ shot Freshly squeezed lime juice
Top up with Soda water (club soda)
Alcohol per serving: 7.9g

Thomas Huhn, Switzerland
Thomas followed the classic punch recipe of 1 sour (lemon juice), 2 sweet (sugar and grenadine syrup), 3 strong (Zacapa 23 rum), 4 weak (soda water) and, as he explained, "a fifth element of spice in the shape of Angostura bitters.

Richard Gonzalez, Dominican Republic
Richard unusually put the soda water in his Planter's Punch first and then added 2 shots Zacapa 23 rum, ½ shot lemon juice, ½ shot lime juice, 1¼ shots sugar syrup and a dash of grenadine. Salvatore found it "very well balanced."

Rosita
Glass: Rocks
Garnish: Orange peel
Method: STIR all ingredients with large ice cubes and strain into ice filled glass.
1 shot Don Julio tequila preferably Blanco
1 shot Campari bitter
½ shot Carpano Punt e Mes sweet vermouth
½ shot Dry vermouth
3 drops Angostura aromatic bitters
Alcohol per serving: 10.6g

Ilias Marinakis, Greece
Ilias used 1½ shots Don Julio Reposado tequila, ¾ shot Campari, ¾ shot Sweet vermouth, 1 shot Dry vermouth and 1 dash Angostura aromatic bitters. Salvatore declared it to be "perfectly balanced"

Mojito (Zacapa 23 version)
Glass: Highball
Garnish: Mint sprig
Method: Place the mint in the bottom of glass. Add lime juice and sugar syrup, muddle and top up with crushed ice. Pour rum and soda. Gently stir.
1⅔ shots Zacapa 23 rum
1 shot Freshly squeezed lime juice
½ shot Sugar syrup (2:1 sugar/water)
8 fresh Mint leaves
Top up with Soda water (club soda)
Alcohol per serving: 7.9g

Timo Janse, The Netherlands
In his Mojita Timo used 1⅔ shots Zacapa 23 rum, ⅔ shot sugar syrup (1:1), 12 mint leaves, ⅔ shot lime juice before topping with soda water. He garnished the drink with five mint sprigs which Salvatore said was "a little too much."

Margarita
(straight up or on the rocks bartender's choice)
Glass: Coupette or rocks
Garnish: Half salt rim
Method: Shake all ingredients with ice and fine strain into coupette glass or over the ice in rock glass.

2 shots Don Julio tequila preferably reposado
1 shot Freshly squeezed lime juice
1 shot Triple sec liqueur
Alcohol per serving: 13.7g

Cosmopolitan
Ketel One Citroen, cranberry juice, triple sec, lime juice.
Glass: Martini
Garnish: Orange peel
Method: Shake all ingredients with ice and fine strain into chilled glass.

2 shots Ketel One Citroen vodka
1 shot Cranberry juice
1 shot Triple Sec liqueur
1 shot Freshly squeezed lime juice
Alcohol per serving: 10.7g

Judge's comments: Salvatore commented that many people use too much cranberry juice in this cocktail. "It should be a lovely pink colour. Too much cranberry makes the drink overly tart and means the spirit has little presence."

Arnaldo Hernandez, Puerto Rico
Arnaldo's recipe consisted of 1 shot Ketel One vodka, ½ shot Triple Sec liqueur, ½ shot lime juice and 2 shots cranberry juice. When asked why he added more cranberry juice than vodka Arnaldo said, "This is my interpretation of the drink as I find more cranberry juice gives the drink a more fashionable colour."

Heinz Kaiser, Austria
Heinz said of his garnish, "If you burn the orange peel, you burn the drink." Salvatore commented, "You have great knowledge, this is the best balanced Cosmopolitan I've tasted."

Singapore Sling (Raffles version)
Glass: Sling
Garnish: Pineapple triangle and cherry
Method: Shake all ingredients with ice and strain into ice-filled glass.

1⅓ shot Tanqueray No. TEN gin
⅓ shot Bénédictine D.O.M. liqueur
⅔ shot Heering cherry brandy liqueur
⅓ shot Triple Sec liqueur
⅓ shot Grenadine syrup
2⅔ shots Pressed pineapple juice
1 shot Freshly squeezed lime juice
3 drops Angostura aromatic bitters
Alcohol per serving: 13.2g

Judge's comments: Salvatore explained that he likes to float the Bénédictine on the surface of his Singapore Slings so the drinker experiences herbal and then fruity flavours.

Max La Rocca, Ireland
Max made his Singapore Sling with 1⅓ shots Tanqueray No. Ten gin, ½ shot cherry brandy, ⅙ shot triple sec, ½ shot lime juice, ⅙ shot Bénédictine liqueur, ⅓ shot grenadine syrup, 3 shots pineapple juice and 2 dashes Angostura aromatic bitters.

Noach Van Damme, Belgium
Noach's Singapore Sling consisted of ½ shot lime juice, 1 shot Tanqueray No. Ten gin, ⅓ shot triple sec liqueur, ⅓ shot Bénédictine liqueur, ½ shot cherry brandy, 4 shots pineapple juice and 2 dashes of Angostura bitters.

Silk Stocking
Glass: Martini
Method: Shake all ingredients with ice and fine strain into a chilled glass.

1½ shots Don Julio Blanco tequila
⅓ shot Grenadine syrup
⅔ shot White crème de cacao liqueur
⅔ shot Double (heavy) cream
Alcohol per serving: 9.1g

Max La Rocca, Ireland
Max made his Silk Stocking using 2 shots Don Julio Añejo tequila, 1 shot cream, 1 shot crème de cacao liqueur and ⅛ shot grenadine.

Bloody Mary

Ketel One vodka and your choice from: pressed tomato juice, black pepper, Worcestershire sauce, Tabasco, sea salt, celery salt, port, fino dry sherry, lemon, lime.
Garnish: Celery, lemon wheel, olive and caper
Method: Pour all ingredients into shaker, fill other tin shaker with ice and mix using a rolling technique. Strain into a highball glass filled with large ice cubes.

1⅓ shots Ketel One vodka
3⅓ shots Pago tomato juice
½ shot Bloody Mary mix*
½ shot Freshly squeezed lemon juice
*Bloody Mary mix: black pepper, 100ml Worcestershire sauce, 10ml Tabasco, Tajin Mexican salt, celery salt, 10ml port, 20ml fino dry sherry, fresh coriander, 50ml soya sauce, fresh horseradish, 1 bar spoon English mustard. Blend all ingredients in food blender and pour into a bottle, store in a refrigerator.
Alcohol per serving: 7.2g

Judge's comments: "A Bloody Mary should be spicy enough to wake you up, give you a jump start. It is a morning restorative drink."

Blood and Sand

Johnnie Walker Gold Label Blended Scotch Whisky, sweet vermouth, cherry brandy, orange juice.
Glass: Martini
Garnish: Cherry
Method: Shake all ingredients with ice and fine strain into a chilled glass.

1 shot Johnnie Walker Gold Label Blended Scotch Whisky
1 shot Antica Formula sweet vermouth
1 shot Heering cherry brandy liqueur
1 shot Freshly squeezed orange juice
Alcohol per serving: 9.5g

Timo Janse, The Netherlands

Timo's Blood and Sand consisted of ⅓ of an orange, ⅔ shot cherry brandy liqueur, 1⅓ shots Johnnie Walker Gold Label Blended Scotch Whisky and 1 ⅔ shots sweet vermouh. Salvatore praised Timo for his interpretation and his excellent knowledge.

Noach Van Damme, Belgium

Noach's Blood and Sand consisted of 1 shot Johnnie Walker Gold Label Blended Scotch Whisky, ⅔ shot cherry brandy liqueur, 1 shot orange juice and ⅔ shot sweet vermouth. Salvatore described the drink as being "perfectly balanced, smooth and velvety". He also said Noach had "great presence behind the bar."

Mulatta Daiquiri

Zacapa 23 rum, Crème de Cacao (dark or white), sugar, lime.
Glass: Coupette
Garnish: Lime peel
Method: Shake all ingredients with ice and fine strain into chilled glass.

1¾ shots Zacapa 23 rum
½ shot Crème de cacao (dark or white)
½ shot Sugar syrup (2:1 sugar/water)
1 shot Freshly squeezed lime juice
Alcohol per serving: 9.4g

Juan Felipe Navarro, Columbia

Juan had not come across this drink in his country and was unsure of the ingredients so Salavtore allowed him to consult his notes. Sadly he built his drink in the glass and then stirred it rather than shaking it.

Judge's comments:"A twist of orange zest brings this drink alive."

Clover Club

Tanqueray No TEN gin, raspberry syrup, sugar (optional), lemon, egg white
Glass: Coupette
Garnish: Float raspberry
Method: Shake all ingredients with ice and fine strain into chilled glass.

1⅔ shots Tanqueray No. TEN gin
3 Fresh raspberries
½ shot Pomegranate syrup
⅝ shot Freshly squeezed lemon juice
⅓ shot Egg white
Alcohol per serving: 9.3g

Judge's comments:Salvatore loved Thomas Huhn's version of this drink and said it was by far the best of the three classics he'd made.

Painkiller
Glass: Tiki mug
Garnish: Pineapple, orange peel, cinnamon stick and nutmeg
Method: Blend without ice and pour into ice-filled tiki mug.

1⅔ shots Zacapa 23 rum
⅚ shot Freshly squeezed orange juice
3⅓ shots Pressed pineapple juice
⅚ shot Pepe Lopez coconut cream
Alcohol per serving: 7.9g

Ilias Marinakis, Greece
Ilias grated nutmeg both into the shaker before shaking his drink and also over the surface drink after straining into the glass.

Aviation
Glass: Coupette
Garnish: Cherry
Method: Shake all ingredients with ice and fine strain into chilled glass.

1⅔ shots Tanqueray No. TEN gin
⅙ shot Crème de violette liqueur
⅓ shot Maraschino liqueur
⅚ shot Freshly squeezed lemon juice
Alcohol per serving: 11.0g

Judge's comments: Several competitors washed their glass with crème de violette liqueur rather than incorporating the liqueur into their recipe and Salvatore commented that crème de violette is "too delicate to merely coat the glass. It should contribute to both the aroma and colour of the cocktail."

Salvatore also said that the Aviation is "one of the most difficult cocktails to achieve a perfect balance of sweet and sour."

El Diablo
Glass: Highball
Garnish: Lime peel
Method: Shake first three ingredients with ice and strain into ice-filled glass. Top up with ginger ale and gently stir.

1⅔ shots Don Julio tequila (any variant)
½ shot Freshly squuezed lime juice
½ shot Crème de cassis liqueur
Top up with Ginger ale
Alcohol per serving: 9.1g

Rina Fermin, Venezuela
Rina's El Diablo consisted of 1½ shot Don Julio Añejo tequila, ½ shot lemon juice, 1 shot crème de cassis liqueur, ½ shot lemon juice, topped with ginger ale. When Salvatore asked Rina which round of the week she found most challenging Rina replied "This one because you are judging."

WINNER
Timo Janse
Door 74, Amsterdam
Netherlands

Judge's comments: "This round is very important, because it doesn't matter how much knowledge a bartender has, if he cannot work efficiently and skilfully with an element of showmanship and interact with the customer, for me he cannot be considered a first class professional bartender."

DIAGEO
RESERVE

WORLD CLASS
BARTENDER
OF THE YEAR
RESULTS

Challenge winners

The World Class challenge winners and the top three places were announced in a glittering ceremony at the classically styled Zappeion, a building in the National Gardens of Athens in the heart of the city – in fact the first building to be erected for the revival of the Olympic Games back in the 1860s.

The splendour of the palace was a fitting end to a fantastic week's activities, placing the judges on one half of the stage, with seven unfilled chairs waiting to be occupied by the challenge winners and an enormous throne waiting for the overall champion. With the front rows of the audience of 400 occupied by the 24 finalists, the evening was hosted by Diageo's global World Class ambassador Spike Marchant.

One by one, the chairs were filled. Here are the results:

Classic Cocktails
Timo Janse
The Netherlands

Judge's comments: "Timo had all the qualities that I was looking for: charm and charisma, he knew how to tell the story behind the drink, he had great command of a bar that was unknown to him, he really managed to make it his own and create well-balanced drinks. Lastly, he used his shaker like a musical instrument – a true entertainer and host."

Canapé Matching
Jordi Otero
Spain

Market Challenge
Do-Hwan Eom
Korea

Judge's comments: "Dohwan stood out as he made himself follow a routine that was probably familiar to his regular day-to-day interaction with a guest. First he greeted me warmly and offered me a hot moist towel; next he presented me with a glass of water and began to explain the special drink he planned to work-up for me; finally, the drink he presented relied heavily on local products. He did what I hoped, he took chances and it paid off: the drink was the tastiest of the whole challenge and served with grace and good humor."

Ritual & Theatre
Max La Rocca
Ireland

Speed & Taste
Heinz Kaiser
Austria

Judge's comments: "Although Heinz had injured his arm, I didn't see any handicap during his routine, and he was one of the fastest in my challenge. And his Zacapa Old Fashioned was totally outstanding – it was like a different drink. That means he is the one who can create great drinks very fast."

Cocktail Mastery
Torsten Spuhn
Germany

Judge's comments: "Drink-wise Torsten made sure to frame his base spirits with complementary flavours, whereas some bartenders tend to mask their primary ingredients, so in this case the Don Julio shone through in both drinks—and that's the way I like my drinks! More than that, though, Torsten is very much a people person, so his personal base spirit shines through his overall personality, too, and it's obvious that he's a man who cares about his guests. Who could ask for more?

The top three

Ultimately, there had to be a final three, and it was clear the results had been a close run thing.

Third place
Max La Rocca
Ireland
"This will make a huge difference to my life and my career – I feel so much more confident. I'm delighted to come in third place and I was certainly not expecting to win the Ritual and Theatre challenge – I went a little bit over time and felt a bit unsure but I guess I delivered on the whole concept.
Overall I think I gave a steady, consistent performance from start to finish."

Runner Up
Do-Hwan Eom
Korea
"I feel so good to be runner-up overall and a category winner – I put it down to very thorough preparation. There's so much I want to take back home to Korea – my World Class cocktails will all be on the list in my bar, and the number one will be the one I made for the Market Challenge."

Diageo Reserve
World Class Bartender of the Year
Erik Lorincz
UK
"This is such a special day in my life – I know being World Class winner 2010 will bring me some fantastic opportunities for the future. During the challenges, I had positive feedback from three of the judges – Salvatore came and shook my hand, so that meant a lot, for example – but the others were very calm and that didn't give me total confidence. Before my name was mentioned, I just felt empty in my heart, my mind, my whole body.
"Now I'm just really happy."

"Being World Class winner really is life changing. My life changed 360-degrees, I've travelled to 15 countries, and learned from so many different bartending cultures and styles. It made me think very differently about bartending, particularly Japan, which made me look more closely at presentation and technical precision.
"My advice to Erik is to be himself and enjoy what he learns – he'll certainly make plenty of new friends around the world."

Aristotelis Papadopoulos,
World Class 2009 winner

"Diageo Reserve Brands is very proud. We have trained 6,000 bartenders in 24 markets around the world. We're proud to spend time with our bartenders, working with such fantastic spirits. The strapline for World Class is 'Raising the Bar': now everyone can raise a glass now to this show of outstanding, quality bartending.

World Class shows customers around the world how our premium spirits contribute to a more enjoyable and more memorable cocktail culture."

**Rudy Paoli,
Global Reserve
Brands General Manager**

THE
GLOBAL
CHAMPION

The Global Champion

Ultimately, there was one contender who stood out from the competition. So what exactly was it that meant he was World Class?

"I've known Erik a long time but I'd never really seen his performance before, and he amazed me. In my challenge, he was fast, tidy and his six drinks were above the standard – and as I say, the Speed and Taste challenge shows what finalists' real daily work is like behind their bar.

"Erik's bartending is fluent and beautiful and he is respectful of his guests for sure. I can certainly say that he is "World Class"."
Hidetsugu Ueno

"Like in any competition, you've got to be really prepared and to have done the ground work – and believe me that was true of most of these ladies and gents. But there is one additional winning quality that sports figures like Roger Federer exhibit in the moment of truth: the ability to relax within the competition and perform with real effortlessness. Erik was in that place during this competition and others simply did not perform that consistently."
Dale DeGroff

"I've known Erik for a few years now, and I've always considered him to be a world class bartender. Above all, Erik knows how to make his guests feel very special, and well looked after – and that's what being a bartender is all about."
Gaz Regan

"Erik is in a class of his own – a real professional who thought about how he set up the bar like a stage in the theatre. He has his own style but also shows his own awareness of the brotherhood of bartending. He smiles, but he is clearly serious in this business, bringing passion and soul behind the bar."
Salvatore Calabrese

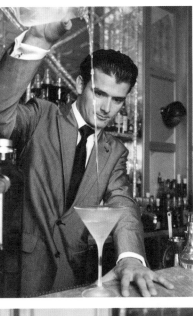

A World Class act: Erik Lorincz

Diageo World Class Bartender of the Year 2010 winner Erik Lorincz personifies the qualities of a modern mixologist. Here, we chart his career and explore what exactly it is that makes him worthy of the title.

Growing up in western Slovakia, in the resolutely beer-drinking culture of his native city Nitra, Erik Lorincz can hardly have predicted that he would one day be crowned king of cocktails in a grand and elaborate ceremony in Greece.

But after the end of a week-long trial by fire in Athens, and a year-long global search for a star bartender, Erik was named Diageo World Class champion 2010 by some of the most influential mixologists in the world. And as they applauded, Erik, clutching his prize, looked quite at home enthroned on the platform in front of an audience of 400.

And rightly so: despite his humble origins, Erik's prize is the product of a passion for the craft of bartending, a passion which has consumed him since he was 18. Now 30-years-old, his career path demonstrates someone who has pursued their dreams to realise their greatest ambitions.

In Erik are exactly the characteristics you would look for in someone to personify the sophistication of modern cocktail culture and mixology.

In his home now in London, his precise Japanese-inspired service techniques and innate theatricality are renowned, while his creativity and flair for producing drinks – both simple serves and molecular drinks – are becoming famous internationally, perfectly illustrated with his Rising to the Sky cocktail, showcased at World Class 2010.

His style and skills are testament to a journey that began back in 1998 when Erik chose a path that was instantly at odds with most of his peers in Nitra – studying hospitality and learning the art of silver service. "My friends wanted to be dirty from oil, not wearing a white shirt, but I loved it. There was just something in my mind that meant I wanted to work with people in this way."

But the path was a rocky one almost instantly, and Erik had to bow out from work – from anything, in fact – because of spinal problems and a slipped disc. Happily, after six months lying flat on his back, he was well enough to start work at his father's insulation business and, crucially for the world of drink, also began working at his local pub.

Here, we get our first glimpse of Erik acting as a host, putting the customer first and taking his job seriously – even though he was simply serving beer. "We served the best beer in Nitra and I learned how to treat the beer properly, and not just in the serve: when we changed every single barrel we would clean the pipes with little sponge balls. We treated it like a golden liquid.

"Each regular had his own glass, and some of them would arrive like clockwork every day. I would have their glass waiting for them when they sat down."

It was while he was working here that he bought a cocktail book for the bar. "There were only beer bars in Nitra but we started practising and making drinks. It was by a German writer, and had 900 cocktails – I remember one called Mexican Roulette. I'm not sure it even had tequila in it."

The local spirits rep, who can't have believed his luck, helped Erik build up a half-decent spirits collection, and further encouraged Erik with the gift of another cocktail book. On the back page was an advert for the R.U. Shop cocktail school in Prague. Slightly sceptical, as he had previously talked to a cocktail school which promised him an 'International Bartending Certificate' after a few days, Erik called the school and was gratified to hear it was a three-month course.

"My parents thought I was crazy. 'There are no cocktail bars in Nitra,' they said. 'What are you going to do when you finish?'"

It took another year for Erik to save up enough money, then armed only with a rucksack, a map of Prague, and looking like any other student with shoulder-length hair, he embarked on a 250-mile bus journey and started bar school.

"My first day, the tutor gave me his book. He told me after three months I would have its 240 recipes in my head. We made some classics: a Rob Roy, I think, maybe a Manhattan and a few others. I remember I couldn't open my shaker. The next day he asked us to repeat the drinks. I was completely lost and I realised I had to take his book seriously. I would go to sleep reading it and wake up with my face in it."

At the time, Erik's tutors were involved in a consultancy project, launching a new cocktail bar in Slovakia. They invited Erik to start work there, so every weekend until the end of his course he would travel from Prague to Bratislava. He was a bar-back but already he outshone his colleagues, and he would whisper cocktail recipes to the bartender as he washed glasses. "He'd say 'Erik, Mai Tai?' and I would tell him how to make it."

From his entire class, only Erik passed the final exams. "The only mistake I made was I didn't upsell vodka. I was so close to a perfect score."

Over the next three years he honed his skills, catering lavish parties for extra cash and fulfilling his obligatory military service too. But it was during his work as a bartender that he came into contact with increasing numbers of English speakers. A visiting American mentioned a hotel in London called the Sanderson, and Erik was intrigued by its Long Bar.

Once again, armed with only a map and a bus ticket, now aged 24, he made his way to England and enrolled in language school for six months, and began visiting bars he had marked on his map. One eluded him, but one night, wandering down Kingly Street in Soho, he discovered it when he saw a queue of glamorous people outside Attica, then London's hottest nightspot.

Erik was shocked at the £20 entry fee, but he and his friend were eventually let in for £15 each. "We walked in, there was this massive bar, and I thought, well, this is something. I hadn't realised it was such a hotspot. I immediately started looking for the bar manager and, in my broken English, told him I was looking for work. He told me to come back tomorrow, and I thought, well, that was easy, no interview! I couldn't even speak English."

The next day, Erik, already an experienced bartender, began as a bus-boy, sweeping the floor and setting up the tables – but secretly he would test his bartender colleagues' abilities. "I would hold up a bottle of Southern Comfort and ask what it was. The bartenders would take it from me, look at the label and read it back to me. At that moment, I knew I would be able to make it as a bartender. I thought to myself: 'I'm going to put you guys in my pocket'."

From bus-boy he was made bar-back, then head bar-back, but after a year-and-a-half, Erik's name disappeared off the rota. Concerned he had lost his job, he found his boss, who actually led him to a station behind the bar.

He was finally a fully-fledged bartender again, albeit with a station hidden behind a pillar.

The next day, the bar manager gathered the team and went through the previous night's takings. Erik's station, despite being behind the pillar, had rung up £5,000 – some £2,000 more than his experienced colleagues with better stations. The next night he was put on the best station, in the middle of the bar, and was fast-tracked to being head bartender.

Unfortunately, Erik tired of serving endless vodka Red Bulls, and when Attica's star faded and it looked like it was going to close, he gave his notice and started at Nozomi, a Japanese restaurant on Beauchamp Place in Knightsbridge (one of Erik's winning World Class cocktails is named after the restaurant). It was here that he began to fully hone his bartending skills: he was given full responsibility for the cocktail list and learned to carve ice.

"I started working with infusions, and sake, really getting into mixology, and I went with a friend to Tokyo. It was exactly what I was looking for. I saw bartending as a fine art – like a silver service waiter, but behind the bar. It was unbelievable – it was not just about cocktails, in fact the drinks were relatively simple, but the service gave you the feeling you were in a five-star hotel. Even if you asked for water, it was a real ceremony, a ritual. I remember spending four hours at Tender bar, just watching Kazuo Ueda make drinks, learning his 'Hard Shake' technique and stirring by barely moving your fingers. Great theatre."

Back in London, and having worked in a pub, a cocktail bar, a club and a restaurant, Erik figured he needed some hotel experience. He landed a job at the Sanderson, the hotel that had led him to the UK.

"I wasn't actually that impressed by the Long Bar but when I went into the Purple Bar it reminded me of Japan. I started polishing my techniques, doing it like an artist. I was not just making the drinks but thinking about how to attract people to drink them. With people really watching how you make a drink, I realised I was on a stage."

The next two years saw Erik attract wider industry attention. He began entering industry competitions, becoming a finalist in Theme magazine's and CLASS magazine's Bartender of the Year national competitions in 2008, and the showman in him really began to come out. Wearing striking outfits and often transporting elaborate equipment – and homemade ice – around the globe, he tends to stand apart from the crowd.

Becoming Diageo World Class champion is the 12th, and biggest, industry competition Erik has won, though he was also nominated in 2008 for Bartender of the Year at New Orleans' Tales of the Cocktail in 2008, alongside some of the biggest names in bartending, including New York's Jim Meehan of PDT, Sam Ross of Milk & Honey and Philip Ward, then at Death & Co.; and his London contemporaries Nick Strangeway, then at Hawksmoor (Nick would go on to win); Charles Vexenat, then at The Lonsdale; and Agostino Perrone, then at Montgomery Place.

It was the professional partnership and friendship that he formed with Agostino that has most recently influenced Erik. Working together at The Connaught, he says their teamwork really helped him develop. "As soon as I walked in to the bar, I thought 'I love this place', but I waited until Ago had signed his contract before I signed up too. Working with him was a perfect match. We did things in different ways but we always knew what the other was doing: we didn't even need to talk to each other. Guests would say it was like watching tennis when we were at the bar together, looking from me, to him, then back again."

Erik likes to work with more complex flavours, especially gin, tequila, whisky and rum, his creativity driven by the desire to give customers an experience to remember. "There are many classics with great stories behind them. I like to recreate them and give them a new style for our age.

"The Connaught didn't want to create a classic bar, but something modern, using Heston Blumenthal-style techniques – though I remember we created the cocktail menu in a windowless room without air-conditioning, not particularly glamorous!"

The bar's ethos perfectly chimed with Erik's style, illustrated by his Muchacha Caliente, otherwise known as a Connaught Bloody Mary, where celery 'air' takes the place of the traditional celery stick. "It has become one of the bar's most iconic cocktails," he says.

Erik has just started the next stage of his bartending journey. He has toasted his colleagues at The Connaught a fond farewell – with an 1893 cognac, no less – and joined the Savoy as head bartender in the famed American bar, recently open again following the hotel's major refurbishment.

If that isn't a major challenge in itself – with some big, Peter Dorelli-sized shoes to fill – his role as Diageo World Class champion will also see him travel around the world as a roving ambassador for Diageo Reserve Brands, passing on his knowledge and skills. For just as his heroes – the World Class 2010 judges – pass on their expertise, so Erik wants to teach others.

Like we said, a World Class act. Congratulations, and good luck for the year ahead.

By Ian Cameron

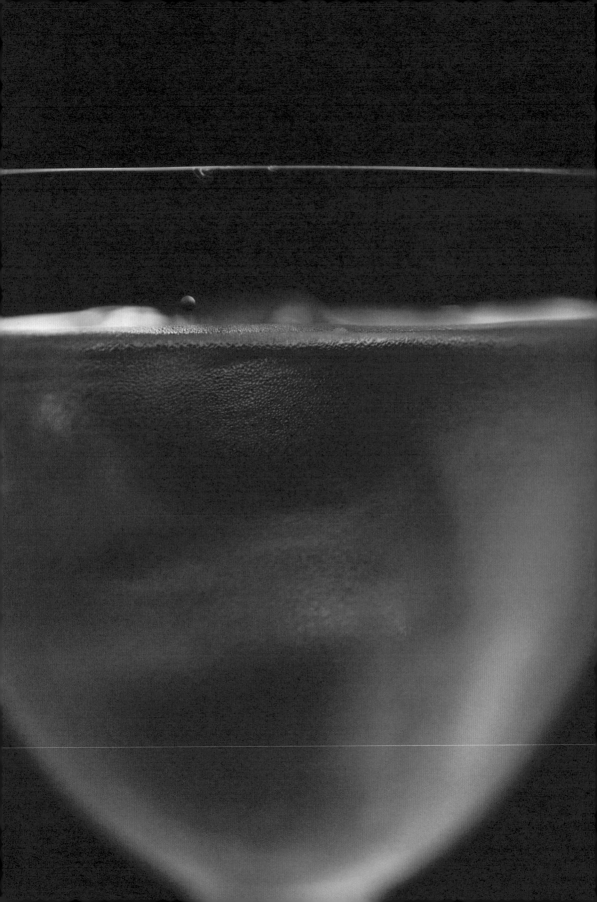

ERIK'S
SIGNATURE
COCKTAILS

Johnnie Walker

Johnnie Walker has grown from humble beginnings to become the world's greatest Scotch whisky house with a reputation for big flavours and expert blends.

In 1820, John Walker, aged just fifteen and the son of an Ayrshire farmer, established the family grocer's business in Kilmarnock where he sold tea, coffee and provisions along with the limited amount of malts that were available to him at the time. His son, Alexander, joined the enterprise a year before his father died in 1857 and dramatically developed the whisky side of the business.

He identified the growing trend towards brands and created the first recognised brand of Johnnie Walker 'Old Highland Whisky' in the 1860s. By the time Alexander's sons joined the business, it was no longer a grocers, but a firm of whisky merchants and it was John Walker's grandsons who in 1908 patented the name Johnnie Walker and launched a White Label, Special Red Label and Extra Special Black Label Whisky. The white was dropped, but the red and black in their easily recognisable square bottles with the 'striding dandy' became internationally successful blends – the red became the world's best-selling Scotch.

Over the next century, John Walker and Sons grew from strength to strength, driven by an uncompromising approach to quality. Under the guardianship of the Walker family, new and distinctive blends were developed to build the brand that is recognised around the world today.

Generations of blending heritage are continued today by the Master Blender, Jim Beveridge and his experienced team. Thanks to Diageo's large and diverse stable of malt whisky distilleries, the blending team can draw from some of the world's most valuable whisky reserves. They work with an unparalleled passion and ability to consistently deliver distinctive and popular blends that set Johnnie Walker apart from other whisky houses.

Malt and grain whiskies are selected from all corners of Scotland and these diverse flavours are brought together at whisky warehouses in Menstrie, where they are blended. The Johnnie Walker 'house' style is 'big flavour', known primarily for its West Coast smoky finish. This house style is reflected throughout the Johnnie Walker range.

Johnnie Walker
Gold Label

This 'Centenary Blend' was inspired by Alexander Walker II's recipe created in 1920 to celebrate the founding of the company by John Walker 100 years before. Gold Label Reserve is blended from specially selected casks that have been set aside by Jim Beveridge, the Johnnie Walker Master Blender. The blend includes Clynelish Single Malt. Gold label is so prized that it was only sold to private customers during the 19th century.

Johnnie Walker
Blue Label

Johnnie Walker Blue Label contains some of the rarest and most exceptional whiskies in the Johnnie Walker reserves, each hand selected for their flavour and character by the Master Blender, Jim Beveridge. Johnnie Walker Blue Label is a commeration of John Walker & Sons 'Old Highland Whisky' from 1867 the blending notes are the basis for the blend today. Casks are selected from each region of Scotland to give the unique complexity and only 1 in 10,000 is deemed good enough for each small batch. Johnnie Walker believe that neither whisky age alone or single location is enough to create this unrivalled masterpiece. The Johnnie Walker Blue Label has a powerful, complex character with layers of fruit, smoke and honey ending with a long intense and smooth finish

Johnnie Walker
Blue Label King George V

Created to celebrate the first Royal Warrant granted to John Walker and Sons Limited to supply Scotch whisky to the British Royal Household in 1934, 'Blue Label King George V' is handcrafted from rare whiskies produced only in distilleries that operated during the reign of King George V, including several Single Malts which no longer exist, including the highly prized Port Ellen.

The John walker

This whisky's direct name is a reference to its celebration of the life of John Walker and the progress of his business from humble grocers to whisky merchants. It is a blend of just nine exceptionally rare whiskies, including irreplaceable casks from the Cambus and Glen Albyn distilleries, handcrafted in single barrel batches of only 330 bottles. Once blended, The John Walker is left to rest in 100-year-old oak casks. This exceptional whisky is presented in a unique, hand-blown and individually numbered Baccarat crystal decanter with 24 carat gold plated neck and bottle stopper. Each decanter nestles in a handcrafted lacquer wooden box that takes sixty man hours to produce.

www.johnniewalker.com

King's Elixir

Glass: Toddy
Garnish: Lemon zest twist
Method: MIX ingredients and then heat using steam wand from espresso machine.
1 slice Fresh ginger root (thumbnail sized)
2 shots Johnnie Walker Blue Label Blended Scotch Whisky
⅚ shot Ginger liqueur
⅔ shot Agave nectar blended with brewed matcha tea (2:1)
3 ⅓ shots Lapsang Souchong tea
1 shot Freshly squeezed lemon juice

Alcohol per serving: 13.5g

Erik's Rob Roy

Glass: Coupette
Garnish: Orange zest twist
Method: STIR all ingredients with ice and fine strain into chilled glass.
1⅚ shots Johnnie Walker Blue Label Blended Scotch Whisky
½ shot Carpano Antica Formula
⅓ shot Gancia Rosso vermouth
⅓ shot Martini Rosso vermouth
3 dashes Angostura aromatic bitters

Alcohol per serving: 11.9g

1 Shot = 15ml / ½ ounce

Tranquility Whisky Smash

Glass: Flute
Garnish: Sprinkle dried peppermint flakes
Method: SHAKE all ingredients with ice and fine strain into chilled glass.
8 fresh Mint leaves
1 ⅚ shots Johnnie Walker Blue Label Blended Scotch Whisky
1 shot Pressed pineapple juice
⅓ shot Yuzu juice
⅔ shot Freshly squeezed lemon juice
½ shot Sugar syrup

Alcohol per serving: 8.7g

SF Julep

Glass: Julep cup
Garnish: Shisho leaves
Method: BUILD in julep cup. STIR vanilla and cherry wine. Add other ingredients, CHURN drink with crushed ice.
1 spoon Vanilla syrup
⅔ shot Visciolata del Cardinale cherry wine
2 fresh Shisho leaves
1 ⅔ shots Johnnie Walker Blue Label Blended Scotch Whisky
3 drops Abbott's bitters
Notes: Named after Sadie Frost who was being photographed in Erik's bar at the same time that we were photographing this drink at the other end of the bar.

Alcohol per serving: 9.0g

Old House Flip

Glass: Tankard
Garnish: Poker seared
Method: Whisk egg yolk, add next three ingredients and THROW between tankards and top with ale; poke with hot poker.
1 Egg yolk
1⅔ shots Johnnie Walker Blue Label Blended Scotch Whisky
½ shots Maple syrup
3 drops Repeal bitters
top with Ale

Alcohol per serving: 10.5g

Golden Fire Bowl

Glass: Flamed sugar cone
Method: Heat first nine ingredients in traditional Feuerzangenbowle. Flame alcohol soaked sugar cone.
Recipe makes 20 drinks
200ml Johnnie Walker Blue Label Blended Scotch Whisky
50ml Johnnie Walker Gold Label Blended Scotch Whisky
50ml Talisker Single Malt Scotch Whisky
200ml Claret wine
300ml Pear cider
80ml Freshly squeezed lemon juice
80ml Freshly squeezed lime juice
80ml shots Mandarin juice
1 Vanilla pod, Cinnamon, cloves, cardamom, orange peel, lemon peel, lime peel
250g Sugar cone

Alcohol per serving: 6.5g

1 Shot = 15ml / ½ ounce

CÎROC

SNAP FROST

VODKA

DISTILLED FROM

FINE FRENCH GR

CÎROC.

Cîroc

Pronounced 'Si-Rock' and launched in the US in February 2003, Cîroc vodka was created by Jean-Sébastien Robicquet, a charismatic Frenchman who grew up between Cognac and Bordeaux, so it is perhaps not surprising that he chose to make his new vodka exclusively from grape spirit, particularly Ugni Blanc, the cognac region's key variety. Jean-Sébastien combines this with Mauzac Blanc, an aromatic wine from the Gaillac region – Cîroc vodka's tall slender bottle is embossed with a cockerel perched on a cluster of grapes to symbolise the Gaillac region and its grape-growing heritage.

The Mauzac Blanc vine buds and ripens late, so early frosts can be a problem but contrary to popular belief, and the presence of the term 'Snap Frost' on the bottle, the grapes used are not left on the vine to freeze before harvesting. Mauzac grapes grow in vineyards outside the village walls of Cordes-sur-Ciel at elevations of some 300m. These 'Highlands of Gaillac'-grown grapes are of much higher quality than those grown by the river at the base of the valley. The name Cîroc vodka combines two French words: 'cîme', meaning summit and 'roche', meaning rock – in reference to their lofty home.

After harvesting the Mauzac grapes are left to 'cold macerate'. This involves the skins and pulp of the grape (the lees) being left to rest together at 0-4°C to concentrate flavours prior to cold fermentation (max 16-18°C). These low temperatures are essential to avoid the need to use sulphite (SO4) – the wine maker's friend but distiller's enemy – as it can produce rotten egg flavours in the final distillate. The wine is then taken to Cognac where it is held under a vacuum at 0-4°C before being distilled continuously, twice, through a copper two-column 15-metre-tall steam injected column still to a strength of 94% alcohol/volume.

Quite separately, in another distillery in Cognac, neutral spirit (96.3% alcohol/volume) made from Ugni Blanc grapes is rectified through four column stills to produce an extremely pure spirit. Ugni Blanc is the main grape used in cognac production due to its low strength (10% alcohol/volume) and high acidity, both perfect properties for distillation. This refined Ugni Blanc neutral spirit is then taken to the distillery where the Mauzac spirit was produced for marrying with the Mauzac distillate.

The quantity of Mauzac distillate blended with the Ugni Blanc neutral spirit varies by vintage but is typically around five percent. This occurs in one of three specially adapted copper pot stills of 2,000 litres capacity – all share the name Susie. Due to the high strength of the spirits used it is impossible to use direct heat as is usual in cognac pot stills so a steam heated coil is used. The onion-shaped-head that is usual in cognac stills is not required and so has also been modified. The final distillate is reduced to bottling strength and 1.8 grams of sugar per litre added, as is common practice in the cognac region, to smooth and concentrate flavours.

www.cirocvodka.com

Suzie

Glass: Coupette
Garnish: Orange twist
Method: STIR all ingredients with ice and fine strain into chilled cocktail glass.
1 ⅓ shots Cîroc vodka
⅙ shot Cognac XO
⅓ shot L'Espirit June liqueur
1 ⅓ shot G-Vine gin
Note: This cocktail is named after the pot still used to make the Cîroc vodka. Erik created this cocktail at La Ribaudière, the noted Michelin 2 star restaurant on the bank of the Charente River in Cognac.

Alcohol per serving: 14.5g

Grape Smash

Glass: Highball
Garnish: Sage leaves and chopped grapes.
Method: SHAKE all ingredients with ice and strain into ice-filled glass.
1½ shots Cîroc vodka
3 fresh Sage leaves
6 fresh Green grapes
2 shots Pressed apple juice
1 shot Freshly squeezed lemon juice
½ shots Rosemary syrup
½ shots Elderflower liqueur

Alcohol per serving: 8.3g

Dream

Glass: Flute
Garnish: None
Method: SHAKE first five ingredients, fine strain into chilled glass and top with champagne.
1 shot Cîroc vodka
⅙ shot Blue Curaçao liqueur
⅓ shot Maraschino liqueur
⅚ shot Pink grapefruit juice
⅙ shot Sugar syrup
top up with Chilled champagne

Alcohol per serving: 12.2g

French Days

Glass: Coupette
Garnish: None
Method: STIR all ingredients with ice and fine strain into chilled glass.
2⅔ shots Cîroc vodka infused with foie gras
½ shot Dry vermouth
⅓ shot Crème de cassis liqueur

Alcohol per serving: 14.3g

Oriental Bond

Glass: Highball
Garnish: Kumquat wedges in drink, mint sprig
Method: MUDDLE first two ingredients in base of shaker. Add next four ingredients; SHAKE with ice and fine strain into ice-filled glass. Float Mandarin Napoleon on top.
3 fresh Kumquats
8 fresh Mint leaves
1½ shots Cîroc vodka
⅚ shot Freshly squeezed lemon juice
½ shots Sugar syrup
1 ⅓ shot Pressed apple juice
½ shots Mandarin liqueur

Alcohol per serving: 9.4g

1 Shot = 15ml / ½ ounce

REPOSADO

TEQUILA
— RESERVA DE —
Don Juli
REPOSADO
100% DE AGAVE

alc. 38% vol.   70

HECHO EN MEXICO
PRODUCCIÓN LIMITADA
0097612

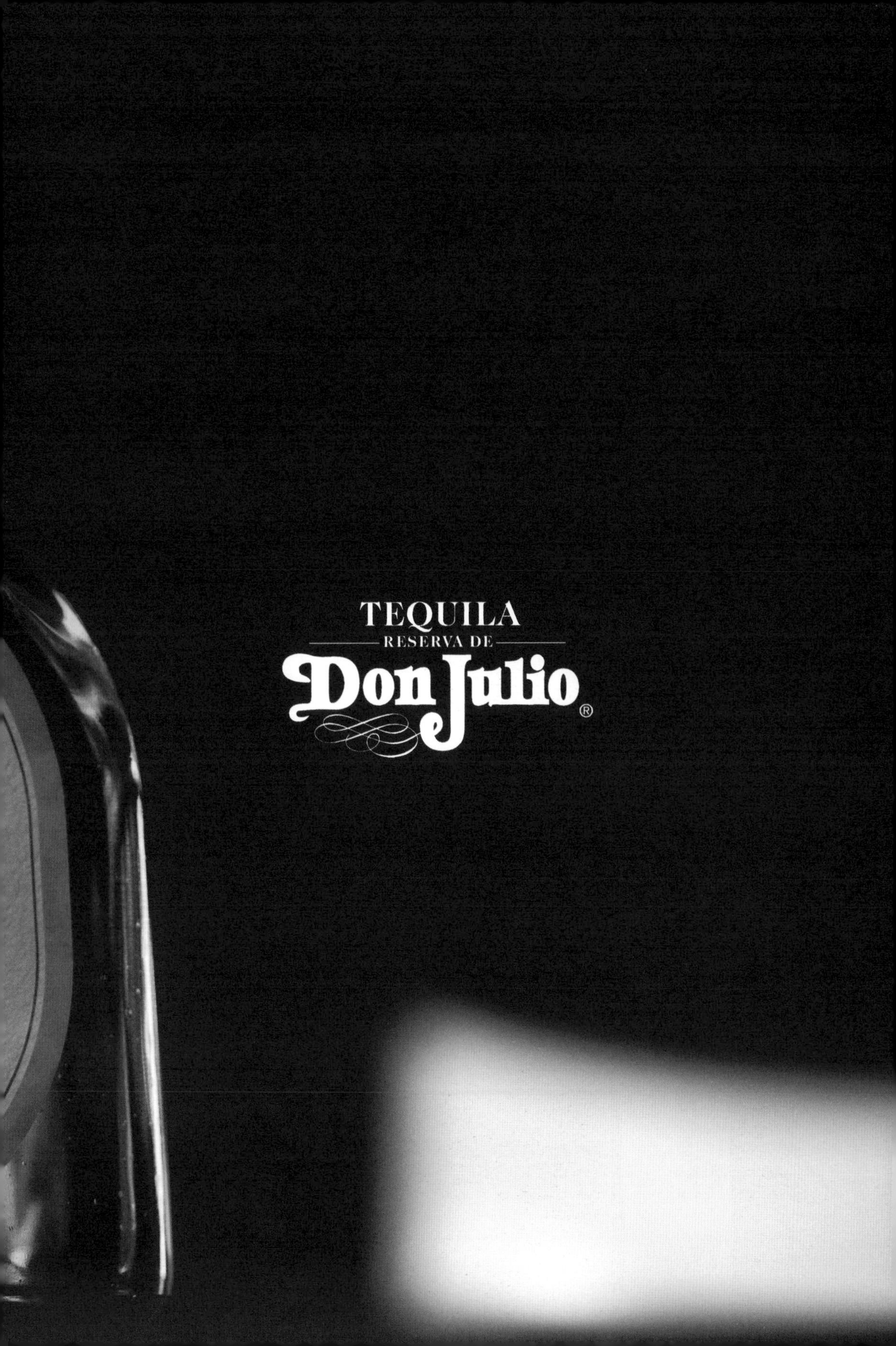
TEQUILA
RESERVA DE
Don Julio®

Don Julio

Today's finest tequilas are recognized among the ranks of other complex and nuanced spirits, as refined and elegant as they are alluring. Whether sipped, savoured or enjoyed in cocktails, tequila has become much more than a spirit reserved for quick shots.

In 1942, at the age of 17, Don Julio González founded his first tequila distillery in his hometown of Atotonilco el Alto. He had spent his youth learning the ancient methods of making mezcal wine and now set about revolutionising tequila production with pioneering agricultural principles, in turn setting the standard for ultra-premium tequila.

The Los Altos region of Mexico offers rich, clay soils and a perfect microclimate for growing the sweet blue agave used in Tequila Don Julio. As one of the oldest tequila makers in the region, Don Julio originally named his tequila Tres Magueyes ("maguey" being another name for the agave plant) and spent the next few decades perfecting his tequila to achieve the highest quality standards, evidenced by his distinct method of planting agave farther apart to yield larger and sweeter plants. With further patience and determination, he cultivated a product worthy of bearing his name.

His artisanal methods are still utilized today and can be seen during the harvest at the estate fields of Tequila Don Julio's distillery, La Primavera. An expert team of jimadors select individual, fully mature agave ripened for eight to 10 years – many other distilleries harvest after only six to seven years – then hand-cut the agave leaves and bitter parts from the 'piñas', ensuring only the sweetest juices are later extracted. The piñas are slowly steam-cooked in masonry ovens for three days and left to rest.

To preserve the characteristic flavour of Tequila Don Julio, the sweet honey juice from the cooked agave is fermented with Don Julio's own proprietary yeast strain.

Master Distiller Enrique de Colsa oversees the small batch, double-distillation process in pot stills, removing the 'head and tail' impurities from the spirit, leaving only the heart of the distillate behind. Three final pot stills of the resulting 100 per cent blue agave tequila are then blended to maintain the consistency of Don Julio's unique taste profile.

Tequila Don Julio Blanco is bottled and immediately released but the aged tequilas – the Reposado, Añejo, 1942 and Real – are matured in American white oak barrels for, respectively, eight months, 18 months, two and a half years and between three and five years.

A testament to Don Julio's dedication to creating only the most premium tequilas, these aged tequilas are matured for longer periods of time than required by the Mexican government.

In 1987, 45 years after Don Julio began his mission of setting the benchmark of excellence for the tequila industry, his sons released a special bottling – Reserva de Don Julio – in his honour. Originally reserved as gifts for friends at a family celebration, his sons made this special tequila tribute available to everyone, officially creating the ultra-premium tequila segment.

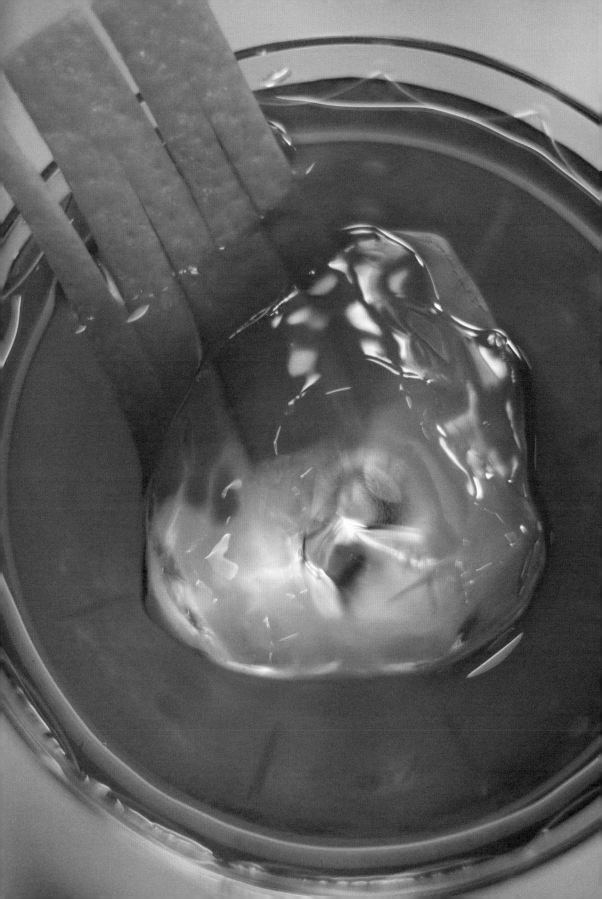

Muchacha Caliente

Glass: Coupette
Garnish: Top with celery air sprinkle with chilli powder
Method: THROW (mix by straining from one vessel to another) all ingredients with ice and strain into chilled glass.
1⅔ shots Don Julio Reposado tequila
⅔ shot Freshly squeezed lime juice
½ shot El Diablo mix (fresh horseradish, fresh coriander, Worchestershire sauce, soya sauce, tajin classico fino dry sherry, naga jolokia chillis, mustard)
3⅓ shots Pego tomato juice
1 pinch celery salt
Notes: The name of this Bloody Mary-styled dink literally translates as 'naughty girl'. To make the celery air add 1 barspoon of Lecite lecithin powder to 500ml freshly extracted celery juice then blend with a hand blender and scoop foam onto surface of the drink.

Alcohol per serving: 6.7g

Martinez

Glass: Coupette
Garnish: Orange zest twist
Method: STIR all ingredients with ice and fine strain into chilled glass.
1 shot Don Julio Reposado tequila
1⅔ shots Carpano Antica Formula
⅓ shot Maraschino liqueur
⅓ shot Galliano Balsamico
3 drops Abbots bitters

Alcohol per serving: 10.5g

Jalisco Sin

Glass: Highball
Garnish: Fig slices
Method: Place tea in hot water and leave to brew.
MUDDLE fig in base of mixing tin; add next 4
ingredients, SHAKE and strain into ice-filled glass.
½ fresh Fig
1½ shots Don Julio Añejo tequila
½ shot Noilly Ambre vermouth
½ shot Vanilla syrup
⅔ shot Freshly squeezed lemon juice
Top with rooibos soda water

Alcohol per serving: 7.8g

Beetroot Margarita

Glass: Coupette
Garnish: Salt rim
Method: POUR balsamico liqueur into cocktail glass
and chill. SHAKE first 4 ingredients with ice and fine
strain into chilled glass.
1½ shots Don Julio Reposado tequila
⅚ shot Triple Sec liqueur
⅚ shot Freshly squeezed lime juice
⅔ shot Fresh Beetroot juice
⅓ shot Galliano balsamico

Alcohol per serving: 12.2g

1 Shot = 15ml / ½ ounce

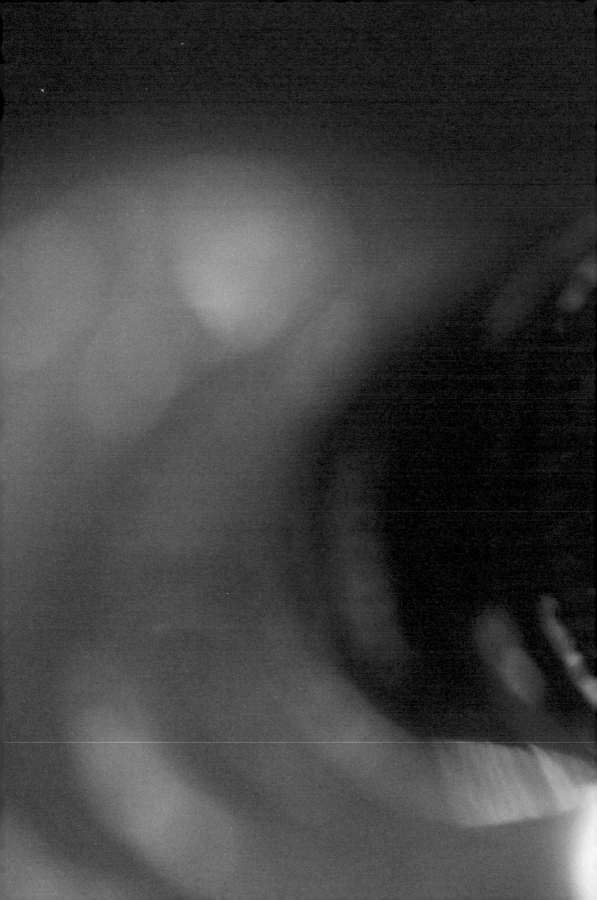

Ketel One

Ketel One® vodka is the creation of Carolus Nolet Sr., who represents the 10th generation of one of Holland's oldest distilling dynasties. The Nolet family has been distilling fine spirits since 1691 when Joannes Nolet started his distillation business in Schiedam, Holland near the North Sea. The Nolet family was one of the first of many distillers to establish themselves in Schiedam, attracted to the area due to its accessibility to shipping, close proximity to water and abundant grain supply. At its peak, Schiedam was home to nearly 400 distilleries and was a recognized centre of spirit distillation. Today, only a handful of distilleries remain.

Ketel One vodka was introduced in the United States in 1983, where it has since enjoyed phenomenal growth. The name Ketel One was inspired by the Dutch word for Pot Still No. 1 (Distilleerketel #1), the nineteenth century alembic copper pot still which is used today in the production of Ketel One vodka at the Nolet Distillery.

Only the finest raw materials are used in the production of Ketel One vodka. Carolus Nolet Sr and his sons Carl Jr and Bob, who both play an integral role in the family business, insist that the production focus is on quality, not quantity. They take immense pride in the production of Ketel One vodka, which combines traditional with modern methods and requires the watchful eye of the master distiller.

Crisp, ultra wheat spirit is partially re-distilled in small batches in ten copper pot stills, one of which is Pot Still No. 1. The early part of this distillate (known as the head) is discarded as too harsh. The final portion (the tail) is discarded as too weak. The remaining copper pot distillate (the heart), with its distinctive roundness and rich mouthfeel, is then charcoal filtered before being combined with a portion of the crisp, silky soft ultra wheat spirit and water. After a 24 hour long rest, the result is a perfectly balanced, crisp and sophisticated ultra premium wheat grain vodka. As a last check, each final production run of Ketel One vodka is approved by a member of the Nolet family.

Ketel One Citroen

Having already created what they, and many top bartenders, consider the perfect vodka for Martinis, the Nolet family wanted to create a flavoured vodka of equal excellence for making the ultimate Cosmopolitan.

The family spent more than two years researching and evaluating different blending and infusion methods, as well as testing numerous samples of citrus essence to arrive at the formula used today.

The vodka is made through the costly, but effective process of hand-crafting small batches of unflavoured vodka which is then infused with natural citrus oils. This results in a complex, yet delicate flavour profile. Expect a refreshing lemon-zest fragrance and flavours of freshly cut lemon with honey sweetness. The vodka is silky soft in the mouth with a sweet honey, and lemon custardy finish.

Ketel One Oranje

Ketel One Oranje was launched on 30 April 2010 to coincide with 'Queen's Day' - a national holiday in the Netherlands which honours the Queen's official birthday. The colour orange represents the Dutch royal family name, The Family Nassau, House of Orange.

Ketel One Oranje is made by flavouring Ketel One vodka with an infusion of Italian Mandarin oranges and Valencia oranges from Florida and Brazil. Expect dry, Satsuma-like flavours with a creaminess that coats the tongue.

The palate is drier than the nose suggests, with a pithy orange quality, a touch of warming spice and a creamy, zesty orange finish.

www.ketelone.com

Cherry Sling

Glass: Sling
Garnish: Mint sprig
Method: SHAKE all ingredients with ice and fine strain into ice-filled glass.
3 fresh Cherries
2 spoons Homemade cinnamon sugar (blend cinnamon stick and caster sugar to fine powder)
1⅔ shots Ketel One vodka
⅓ shot Lemon & yuzu juice mix (2:1)
⅔ shot Freshly squeezed lemon
1⅔ shots Pressed pineapple juice
⅚ shot Cherry wine
Top up with Ginger ale

Alcohol per serving: 9.3g

Spring Garden

Glass: Collins
Garnish: Mint sprig and raspberry
Method: SHAKE all ingredients with ice and strain into ice-filled glass.
1½ shots Ketel One vodka
½ shots Sugar syrup
⅚ shot Freshly squeezed lemon juice
2⅔ shots Pressed apple juice
3 fresh Raspberries
8 fresh Mint leaves

Alcohol per serving: 7.1g

Russian Cup

Glass: Small tankard
Garnish: Cucumber spiral, lime wedge, ginger slice
Method: SHAKE first five ingredients with ice and
strain into cracked ice-filled tankard, top with
champagne.
3⅙ shot Ketel One vodka
⅓ shot Ginger syrup
⅔ shot Freshly squeezed lemon juice
3 drops Aromatic bitters
⅔ shot Sweet vermouth
top up with Chilled champagne

Alcohol per serving: 18.8g

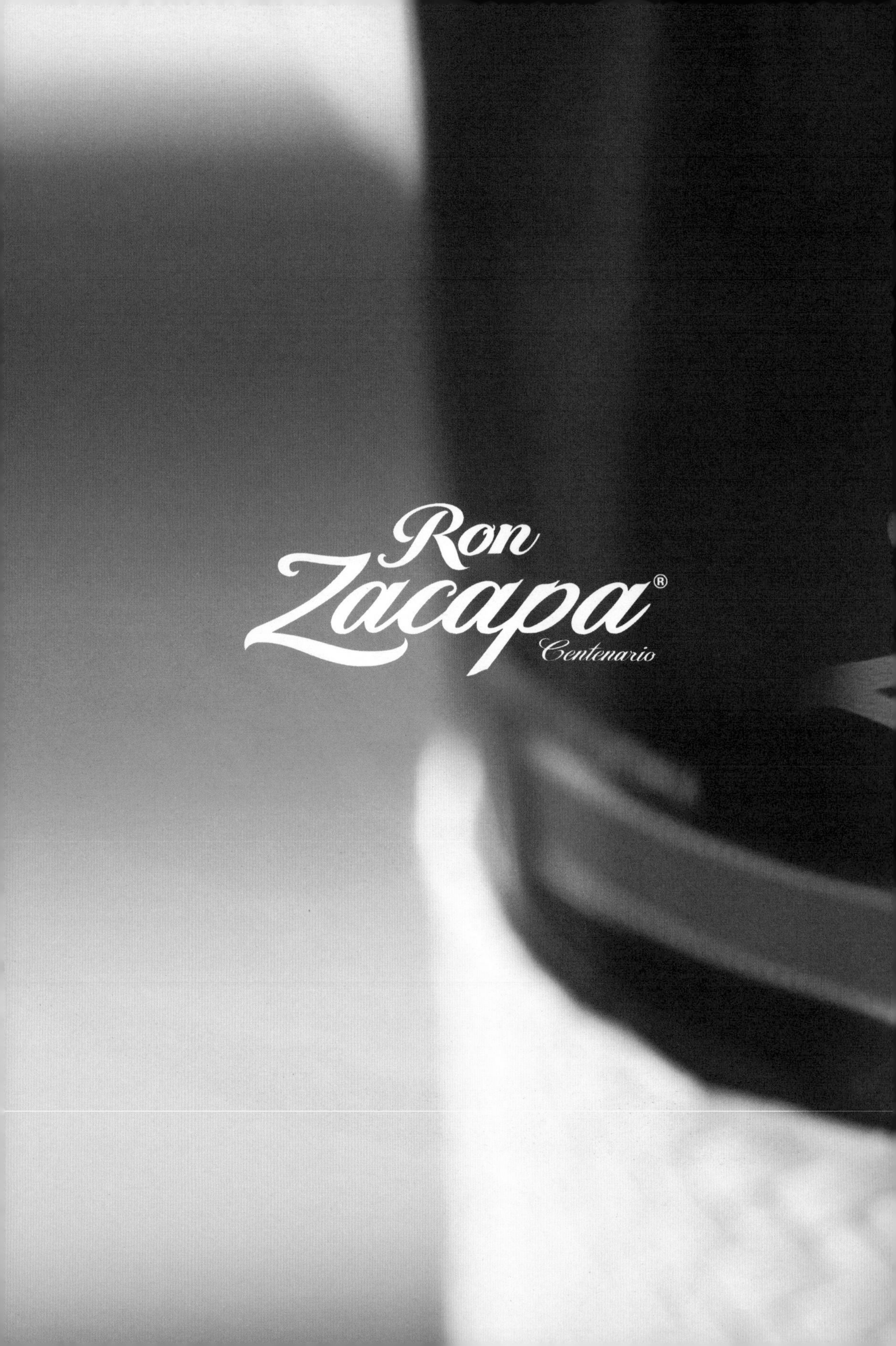
Ron
Zacapa®
Centenario

Ron Zacapa® Centenario

The Ron Zacapa distillery sits 2,300 metres (one and a half miles) above sea level in the shadows of soaring Guatemalan mountains and active volcanoes. Unusually, instead of being made from molasses (as is the case with most rums) Zacapa rum is produced from the concentrated first pressing of sugar cane juice, referred to as 'virgin sugar cane honey'. It is also set apart from other rums by a unique and complex Solera maturation process.

Barrels previously used to age American whiskey, sherry, and Pedro Ximenez wines are used in a multi-stage ageing process during which there is repeated reblending with very old aged rums introduced at each stage of the blending process. Scrapping and recharging of casks also plays an important part in this maturation process which concludes in a final marrying vat. This process takes place in the 'House Above the Clouds' perched at 2,300 metres (7,650 ft) above sea level, so unusual atmospheric conditions are also at play. Depending on the variant, the final product in each bottle is a blend of rums aged between 6 and 23 years for Zacapa 23 rum, and 6 to 25 years for Zacapa XO.

Ron Zacapa is presented in a bottle made distinctive by a Petate band, an ancient royal Mayan symbol. This is made from hand-woven palm leaves prepared by a group of local women in Guatemala. However, it is the flavour of Zacapa rum that really sets it apart with its hugely complex palate appearing slightly sweet while giving rich notes of coffee, roast chestnut, smoky wood and tobacco. Incredibly, for such a well-aged rum, Zacapa is also wonderfully fruity with notes of cherry and sweet molasses.

Tom & Jerry & Erik

Glass: Tom & Jerry bowl and cups
Garnish Grate nutmeg over each cup
Method: WHISK the egg yolks with muscovado sugar in the Tom & Jerry bowl. Separately BEAT egg whites (helps if you add a splash of hot water). Add other ingredients to bowl and then add beaten egg white and FOLD onto mix. Add large block of ice to bowl. Serve by ladling mix into cups and then grating nutmeg over each.
2 spoon Muscovado sugar (6 spoons)
1 fresh Egg yolks beaten separately (4 eggs)
½ shot Pimento Dram liqueur
3 drops Jerry Thomas decanter bitters
1⅔ shots Zacapa 23 rum
1⅔ shots Spiced Milk (infusion cardamom, ginger, nutmeg, clove, peppercorns)
1½ shot Pampero rum
Mixed in Tom and Jerry bowl
Large block of ice

Alcohol per serving: 16.9g

Navy Officers Punch

Glass: Collins
Garnish: Seasonal fruit
Method: SHAKE all ingredients with ice and strain into ice-filled glass. (Multiply recipe as appropriate to fill punch bowl.)
1⅔ shot Zacapa 23 rum
1 shot Port wine
½ shot Batavia arak
⅚ shot Triple Sec liqueur
1 shot Freshly squeezed lime juice
1 shot Pressed pineapple juice
⅔ shot Almond (orgeat) syrup
2 fresh Passion fruit
1 dash Angostura aromatic bitters

Alcohol per serving: 17.5g

Admiral's Nightcap

Glass: Tiki mug
Garnish: Cinnamon stick & lime zest
Method: SHAKE all ingredients with ice and strain into ice-filled tiki mug. Top with crushed ice.
1⅔ shots Zacapa 23 rum
½ shot Velvet Falernum
⅓ shot Pimento Dram liqueur
⅓ shot Agave nectar
2 shots Pressed apple juice
1 shot Freshly squeezed lime juice

Alcohol per serving: 9.4g

Love Me Flip

Glass: Goblet
Garnish: Grate Tonka bean over drink
Method: BEAT egg yolk with sugar in base of shaker. Add other ingredients, SHAKE with ice and fine strain into chilled glass.
1 fresh Egg yolk
1 spoon Caster sugar
1⅔ shots Zacapa 23 rum
⅚ shot Bols Natural Yoghurt liqueur
⅔ shot Pedro Ximénez sherry
3 drops Repeal bitters
Notes: The grated Tonka bean adds a vanilla aroma to the surface of the drink.

Alcohol per serving: 11.9g

1 Shot = 15ml / ½ ounce

Pacaya

Glass: Goblet
Garnish: None
Method: FROTH soya milk, SMOKE with cherry wood. Add first 3 ingredients in glass then LAYER with soya milk froth.
1 shot Zacapa 23 rum
⅓ shot Vanilla syrup
2 shots Kopi Luwak coffee
Soya milk smoked with cherry wood

Alcohol per serving: 4.7g

Alegria

Glass: Toddy
Garnish: Grated nutmeg
Method: POUR all ingredients into warmed glass and STIR.
1 shot Zacapa 23 rum
⅔ shot Pampero Aniversario Reserva Exclusiva
2 spoon Alegria mix*
5 shots Hot water
⅓ shot All spice dram liqueur
3 drops Stoughton's bitters
*Alegria mix: Rapadura sugar, butter, honey, maldon sea salt, pepper
Note: The name was inspired by a song from Cirque du soleil.

Alcohol per serving: 9.5g

Tanqueray®

Nº TEN™

Nº

T

E

N

Tanqueray No. Ten

Tanqueray No. TEN gin was introduced in 2000, designed to bring a new level of luxury to the Martini market. Differentiated from Tanqueray gin, it is the only gin distilled with handpicked fresh fruit and botanicals and its distillation includes use of a small batch pot still named Tiny Ten, after which the gin is named.

The production process is deliberately long and considered and begins with Master Distiller Tom Nichol heading a nosing panel in late summer to assess the quality of botanicals available from around the world – as well as the gin's signature juniper, the mix includes fresh white grapefruit, orange, lime, coriander and a hint of chamomile.

From late August, botanical samples start to arrive and Tom leads a second assessment – only those accepted at this stage are purchased. When shipments begin arriving in the country, the botanicals are put into storage to mature and after a period of time they are ready for distillation.

Into the Tiny Ten still is added the purest grain neutral spirit, demineralised water from a local bore hole, and the grapefruits, limes and oranges, along with some other botanicals. Only the heart from this first distillation is used.

A larger still is now prepared for the main distillation. Known as Old Tom, it has been in continuous use since the reign of King George III. Botanicals including juniper, coriander, angelica and chamomile are added along with more grain neutral spirit, demineralised water and, of course, the heart from the small distillation.

Steam is gently added to the still via a steam coil and after about an hour the infused vapours are ready to be condensed into the initial part of the distillation. The liquid is nosed constantly at this stage to ensure that only the 'heart' of the distillation is used in Tanqueray No. TEN gin – that means the product run is extremely small compared to other gins, but this is absolutely desirable for the quality required from this luxury gin.

www.tanqueray.com

Ringing the Bells

Glass: Coupette
Garnish: Rhubarb air on the side
Method: STIR all ingredients with ice and strain into chilled glass. Add one chunk of ice.
1 ⅔ shots Tanqueray No.TEN gin
⅔ shot Aperol bitter
½ shot Fino dry sherry
2 drops Camomile bitters
Notes: When you pick up the glass to drink, the cube of ice in the glass clunks on the side so ringing the bell. To make the rhubarb air add 1 barspoon of Lecite lecithin powder to 500ml freshly extracted rhubarb juice then blend with a hand blender and scoop foam onto surface of the drink.

Alcohol per serving: 11.1g

Pear-Cha (Japanese for tea)

Glass: Coupette
Garnish: Rosemary sprig
Method: MUDDLE pear in base of shaker. Add other ingredients, SHAKE with ice and fine strain into chilled glass.
¼ fresh Pear
1⅔ shots Tanqueray No.TEN gin infused with Masha tea powder
½ shot Rosemary syrup (2:1 with rosemary sprig infused)
⅚ shot Freshly squeezed lemon juice
⅙ shot Calvados
⅚ shots Pressed apple juice
½ fresh Egg white
Notes: Rosemary and pear are a great flavour combination.

Alcohol per serving: 10.1g

Umami

Glass: Flute
Garnish: Coral crusta (blue curaçao & salt rim)
Method: SHAKE all ingredients with ice and fine strain into chilled glass.
1⅔ shots Tanqueray No.TEN gin
1 shot Pink grapefruit juice
½ shot Freshly squeezed lemon juice
½ shot Triple Sec liqueur
⅙ shot Maraschino liqueur
⅓ shot Sugar syrup

Alcohol per serving: 12.3g

Tanqueray No.Ten Martini

Glass: Martini
Garnish: Lemon zest twist
Method: STIR all ingredients with ice and strain in chilled glass.
3 shots Tanqueray No.TEN gin
½ shot Noilly Prat dry vermouth
3 drops Homemade pink grapefruit & cardamom bitters
Notes: Preferably served from Erik's Tanqueray No. Ten martini trolley.

Alcohol per serving: 17.9g

1 Shot = 15ml / ½ ounce

Erik's Fizz

Glass: Highball
Garnish: Drops of Angostura on top
Method: SHAKE first five ingredients with ice, strain into ice-filled glass and top with soda.
1½ shots Tanqueray No. Ten gin
1 shot Yoghurt liqueur
⅚ shot Freshly squeezed lemon juice
⅔ shot Sugar syrup
½ fresh Egg white
top up with Soda water (club soda)
2 dashes Angostura aromatic bitters

Alcohol per serving: 10.9g

Mr Darcy

Glass: Absinthe
Garnish: None
Method: Brew earl grey tea. MUDDLE cardamom pods, add next 5 ingredients and heat; place absinthe soaked sugar cube on absinthe spoon on top of drink and ignite.
1 shot Earl grey tea
2 dried Cardamom pods
1 shot Tanqueray No. Ten gin
1 shot Lillet Blanc vermouth
1 shot Pink grapefruit juice
⅚ shot Freshly squeezed lemon juice
3 drops Peychaud's aromatic bitters
⅚ shot Absinthe
1 sugar cube

Alcohol per serving: 15.1g

Croquet Club Cobbler

Glass: Goblet
Garnish: Lemon peel, mint sprig, raspberry
Method: MUDDLE pineapple in mixing tin, Add other ingredients; SHAKE with ice and fine strain into cracked ice-filled glass.

1½ shots Tanqueray No. Ten gin
3 drops Rhubarb bitters
⅔ shot Freshly squeezed lemon juice
1 spoon Caster sugar
½ shots Fino dry sherry
⅔ shot Elderflower liqueur
2 Pineapple chunks

Alcohol per serving: 11.0g

Diageo has a long tradition of supporting and promoting responsible drinking amongst customers who serve its liquids. It recognises that consumers want to make informed choices about what they drink on the basis of facts. Diageo's world class marketing code sets the standard for how we communicate with all levels of the retail chain and consumers regarding our products. It is core to Diageo's work that trade and consumers not only appreciate the quality of our products but are able to also serve and consume them responsibly. The key to serving and drinking responsibly is to understand and keep track of how much alcohol is in the beverage being consumed. When promoting drink recipes, we therefore include liquid measures and total alcohol content in grams of alcohol expressed per serving. This has been footnoted across the book where one serving per person equals 24 grams of alcohol.

For more information on responsible drinking visit DRINKiQ.com.